an explorefaith.

# A PEN
# *and* A PATH

*Writing as a Spiritual Practice*

SARAH STOCKTON

Morehouse Publishing, P.O. Box 1321, Harrisburg, PA 17105
Morehouse Publishing, The Tower Building, 11 York Road, London SE1 7NX

Morehouse Publishing is a Continuum imprint.

Cover art courtesy of Superstock
Cover design by Laurie Klein Westhafer

Library of Congress Cataloging-in-Publication Data

Stockton, Sarah.
   A pen and a path : writing as a spiritual practice / by Sarah Stockton.
      p. cm.
   Includes bibliographical references (p.      ).
   ISBN 0-8192-2119-8 (pbk.)
   1. Christian literature—Authorship. 2. Spiritual life—Christianity. I. Title.
   BV4509.5.S847 2004
   248.4—dc22
                                             2004013672

**Printed in the United States of America**

04 05 06 07 08 09  10 9 8 7 6 5 4 3 2 1

# CONTENTS

## PART I: CHOOSING THE PATH OF WRITING AS A SPIRITUAL PRACTICE

## PART II: BEGINNING THE JOURNEY

### Section 1: Reading the Map

### Section 2: Using the Compass: My Religious Tradition and My Relationship with God

**Section 3: Milestones on the Path**

**Section 4: Recognizing and Navigating the Landscape of Experience**

**Section 5: Companions on the Path**

**Section 6: Mapping the World of Work**

# PART III: FOR FURTHER EXPLORATION

# ACKNOWLEDGEMENTS

Thanks to Debra Farrington for giving me the opportunity to write this book. Having to articulate what I believe about the process of approaching God through writing was a spiritual practice in itself. I also want to thank Ryan Masteller, and the rest of the team at Morehouse for creating such a beautiful framework for the words found herein. A special gratitude for everyone who encourages the spiritually infused creative process in others. To everyone who courageously explores the horizons and depths of God's love through creativity: may we all continue to take a joyful leap into the mystery.

explorefaith.org books
# An Introduction

The book you hold in your hand says a lot about you. It reflects your yearning to forge a deep and meaningful relationship with God, to open yourself to the countless ways we can experience the holy, to embrace an image of the divine that frees your soul and fortifies your heart. It is a book published with the spiritual pilgrim in mind through a collaboration of Morehouse Publishing and the Web site explorefaith.org.

The pilgrim's path cannot be mapped beforehand. It moves toward the sacred with twists and turns unique to you alone. Explorefaith.org books honor the truth that we all discover the holy through different doorways, at different points in our lives. These books offer tools for your travels—resources to help you follow your soul's purest longings. Although their approach will change, their purpose remains constant. Our hope is that they will help clear the way for you, providing fruitful avenues for experiencing God's unceasing devotion and perfect love.

www.explorefaith.org

# SPIRITUAL GUIDANCE FOR
# ANYONE SEEKING A PATH TO GOD

A non-profit Web site aimed at **anyone** interested in exploring spiritual issues, explorefaith.org provides an open, non-judgmental, private place for exploring your faith and deepening your connection to the sacred. Material on the site is rich and varied, created to highlight the wisdom of diverse faith traditions, while at the same time expressing the conviction that through Jesus Christ we can experience the heart of God. Tools for meditating with music, art, and poetry; essays about the spiritual meaning in popular books and first-run films; a daily devotional meditation; informative and challenging responses to questions we have all pondered; excerpts from publications with a spiritual message—all this and more is available online at explorefaith.org. As stated on the site's "Who We Are" page, explorefaith.org is deeply committed to the ongoing spiritual formation of people of all ages and all backgrounds, living in countries around the world. The simple goal is to help visitors navigate their journey in faith by providing rich and varied material about God, faith, and spirituality. That material focuses on a God of grace and compassion, whose chief characteristic is love.

You have this book, now try the Web site. Visit us at *www.explore faith.org*. With its emphasis on God's infinite grace and the importance of experiencing the sacred, its openness and respect for different denominations and religions, and its grounding in the love of God expressed through Christianity, explorefaith.org can become a valued part of your faith-formation and on-going spiritual practice.

# Note from the Author

This book is called *A Pen and a Path,* not *A Keyboard and a Path.* Many people will do these exercises in an in-person workshop setting, so computers are not practical. That said, I always use a keyboard when I can— my hand cannot keep up with my thoughts, and I find that I enter in a stream of consciousness mode much more easily when I am not noticing how tired my hand is getting. Some of this is because I'm left-handed, and the method of handwriting that I learned is not very comfortable over the long haul. In my experience, if there is a psychological difference between handwriting and keyboarding, then it's probably purely subjective. All this to say, write in the way that is most comfortable to you. When you are working on your own, and if you have access to a pen and journal as well as a computer, then whatever method minimizes the mechanical aspect of writing is the best, whether that be handwriting or keyboarding. The important thing is to be able to get beyond being too aware of the mechanics of physically writing, into the realm of pure creative thought and spirit connection. Some people can't type and hate computers, so handwriting is better, but if keyboarding helps you get past noticing that you are writing, then choose that.

# INTRODUCTION

One day a woman sits down near a window and opens a spiral, lined notebook she purchased earlier that morning at the grocery store. As she gazes out the window, a bird lands nearby and begins to build a nest in a cozy and safe corner of the railing that surrounds the porch. Over the course of the next few hours, encouraged by the bird's persistent energy and activity, the woman begins to write. Just as the bird builds a nest with grass and twigs and mud as a container for new life, so the woman creates with words a container to hold and sustain her own life. Asking God to be present as she writes, she weaves her dreams, her intentions, her fears, her sorrows, and her greatest joy into a home for her overflowing spirit. The raw materials of her life become a nest, and the nest becomes both a container for her life so far, and a place from which to continue the journey forward.

Within the pages of this book, you are invited, through writing the ongoing story of your own life, to engage in a conversation with God as you weave together the themes, experiences, insights, and feelings that are the precious materials of your spiritual life so far. Using writing in this way, as a spiritual practice, also helps guide the course for the spiritual journey ahead.

Therapists, friends, teachers, workshop leaders, spiritual directors, or pastoral counselors often suggest journaling as a tool for exploring how we feel about our life, our relationships, our religious beliefs, or our spirituality. The concept of "journaling" is a vague proposition at best, which, embarked on without guidance or structure, can result in feelings of depression, aimlessness, and frustration. The spiritual explorer can find herself wandering a path that feels too isolating or meaningless. I hope that you'll find this book to be a welcome companion on your journey, and a resource that provides direction that goes beyond the ill-defined imperative to "journal."

When writing is practiced as a means to an end and not just an end in itself, it becomes a form of articulated prayer. The writer practices clarity, understanding, compassion, and non-judgment toward herself as she writes, just as she receives these gifts in her continuing prayer practice.

If you are a spiritual seeker who wants to write as part of your faith journey, or if you want to go beyond keeping a daily diary format, this book is for you. Each chapter in Part II of the book provides a framework for considering and writing about the events and seasons of your life with others and with the Sacred, by whatever name you call it. If you've never written about your spiritual life before, you'll find help with questions such as: Where should I begin? How do I go about exploring and articulating the themes and images that permeate my life? How can my experiences, both conscious and unconscious, be transformed by the words I choose? Can writing help me to reassess my definition of God and/or my relationship with God? What happens in my relationship with God when I prayerfully write? Long-time practitioners of the art of journaling will also find suggestions that can deepen their experience.

Social scientists have studied the effectiveness of journaling as a means of healing, both emotionally and physically. The most famous studies, by the clinical psychologist James Pennebaker, demonstrate that *narrative* writing is the key to real transformation. Simply writing down our raw feelings tends only to reinforce the feelings, not help us move beyond them. Writing about our lives from a technical point of view ("Today I had a business meeting, went to lunch where I ate a hamburger, went home, cleaned the house") removes us from the story of our lives, turning us into mere spectators. When the two writing approaches are combined, according to Pennebaker, our stories become narratives with plot, purpose, themes, and meaning. By articulating our emotions and narrating the larger story of our lives, we claim that story, instead of feeling like the story is running away with us and we are just along for the ride. We can immerse ourselves in the details without losing perspective, just as we can view ourselves and our lives objectively, without losing a sense of our personal experience.

Writing can also be a powerful and achievable means of discovering more about ourselves as spiritual beings with a graced history. While there aren't clinical studies on the effectiveness of asking God to be present when we write, or of writing to God, knowing God is listening and sharing in our story, the world's spiritual literature is full of those who have found writing to God an important experience. From Augustine's *Confessions* to Rumi's poetry, God is met on the journey of spiritual writing. In the following pages the effectiveness of a narrative approach is intertwined with the belief that writing with spiritual intention and a focus on asking God to witness our story graces us with new awareness and insight. We learn to trust our own experience as we write into the heart of our stories and experience the transformation therein.

This approach comes out of personal experience both as a writer, a spiritual director, and as someone who teaches writing as a spiritual practice. In my book *Restless in Christ: Answering the Call to Spiritual Commitment*, I narrated the story of my journey toward becoming a spiritual director. Writing the book became as much a part of my spiritual transformation as any prayer. As I wrote my way into the mystery of my experience with God, I entered this mystery on two levels: the conscious level of trying to articulate the experience for myself as well as for others, and the subconscious level of being in God's presence as I wrote. I had the very clear sense that God was present and listening throughout that process. I say this because of the transformational effects experienced in my life and relationship with God, and with Christ, that occurred in the moments, days, and months of the writing process. My faith and trust grew, I felt at peace, and my awareness of others became more compassionate. From a writer's perspective, I know God was present because I wrote better than I believe I could have written without God's help. In this way I entered a process of *cocreating* with God the ongoing spiritual transformation of my life story. Just as God's love allows us to love beyond our own human capacity, writing in the light of God brings the gifts of deeper insight, the words we seek, and the courage we need to stay the course and live the truth.

PART I

Choosing the Path of Writing
as a Spiritual Practice

*E*ach chapter in this book contains a short essay on a particular topic, followed by five exercises (outlined below) that guide and encourage your own participation and reflection on the chapter. You'll find it helpful to read the explanations so you're familiar with the basic steps before you begin using them. Work through any or all of the chapters in the book in any order that makes sense to you. When you choose to work through a given chapter, I encourage you to follow all the suggestions. These suggested steps of thinking about, sketching, and then writing about a topic in a heartfelt way are designed to help you move more fluidly and confidently through the process.

## How to Structure Your Writing Time

These chapters and suggested exercises are designed to be helpful either as a self-study guide or in a group setting such as a retreat or workshop. If you are working through the exercises in this book in a group setting, then discussing how much time to spend on writing, on shared, silent reflection time, and on group sharing will depend on the availability and desires of each member. One or two chapters per group meeting would allow enough space for everyone to explore fully the material, through writing and through sharing. A group of more than five or six people might want to divide into smaller groups for sharing. The larger group could then reconvene at the end of the meeting for final reflections. If you are working through this book on your own, then consider what amount of time might work best for you. Some people write best in the morning, and will choose a chapter a day to write about, mulling over and reflecting on what they felt and what they wrote, as they go about the rest of their day. Your schedule might allow for several days in a row of writing, or just one day a week, or one day a month. Others might wish to set aside a whole day, in order to have time to write on several topics. Only you can know how much time you will need for writing, reflection, and further contemplation of the experience. I have found in my own experience that two or three chapters at most over the course of a few hours is plenty, given the in-depth nature of the exercises. Ultimately, there is no one "right" way to approach these exercises. It's important to pay attention to how you are feeling as you work through them: are you feeling rushed? Then you might want to slow down the pace. Are you losing momentum between topics? Then you might want to set aside a longer block of time for a more sustained engagement.

After each writing session, take some time, even a few moments, to contemplate your experience in silence. As you work through these exercises, remember to breathe, to check in with yourself about how you are feeling physically, and to be open to God's presence.

Conversation and reflection on what you've written with a group, a healing professional, or someone in ministry can be enormously illuminating and helpful. While writing is a solitary experience, we are not alone on our path when we write to God. Reflecting on these experiences with another enhances our journey even more. And while writing can be part of the personal, spiritual path, sharing that writing with someone else or in a group helps us grow in spiritual companionship and community.

Ultimately, the practice of writing, when focused on the spirit, becomes both a means of moving inward to the authentic self and outward from our immediate perspective toward a mutual relationship with God. I hope you will find that *A Pen and a Path* offers you useful guideposts along the way.

# How to Use This Book

## Reflection

Each chapter opens with a segment that suggests ways to begin thinking about the topic being addressed. You may choose to reflect on the topics as you go about your day, and return to the writing portion of the chapter later. Alternately you may wish to find a quiet place where you will be uninterrupted and give yourself time to contemplate the material at that moment. Allow yourself to move more completely into your own mindful awareness, as you bring these thoughts to God. Do this by focusing your attention on the present, letting go as best you can of present worries, concerns, and distractions. If there is a ritual that you use to signal a time of prayer or meditation, I invite you to begin with that. You might light a candle, or say a prayer, or simply spend a few minutes with your eyes closed, in silence.

## Pen in Hand

After this period of reflection you are invited to begin writing. The questions and suggestions here provide guidelines to articulating your feelings, thoughts, and awareness in writing. Suggestions may include prompts such as making lists, naming feelings, or writing brief sketches or timelines and the like. Set aside a minimum of fifteen minutes to complete this section. You may always write more, but try to write for at least fifteen minutes, even if some of that time is spent in prayer. Staying with the experience often proves fruitful, even if nothing seems to be happening.

## Noticing

Next, take some time to reflect on your writing. A few questions are provided to get you started in noticing what feelings you had about the writing experience and what you've written. This step is offered as a time to reflect rather than write, but if you feel moved to write your responses, feel free to do so.

## On the Path

The next step involves writing more deeply about the chapter's topic, using what you've written about and discovered already. I'll provide suggested starting places for writing more deeply, but you are free to write in other directions if those seem more fruitful to you. Set aside a more significant amount of time to complete this section in a deeply creative way. I suggest a minimum of thirty minutes. Allow yourself breaks as needed to gaze around the room, stretch, or take a drink of water if you need to, but try not to leave the space you are in, either mentally or physically. Even if you feel finished before the thirty minutes is up, stay with the work. Something may yet arise.

## Contemplation

Finally, spend some time in contemplation of the feelings, thoughts, and inner movements that you have become aware of as a result of these exercises. Then allow yourself time to relax in the quiet of creative energy well-spent, of an exploration bravely accomplished, and the healing support of God's presence, as you rest for awhile on your spiritual journey. Notice any feelings, images, or physical sensations that arise.

Write about these feelings, images, or physical responses if you wish, without concerning yourself with narrative, or even full sentences. A poem may arise, or a simple drawing or sketch. Think of it as a winding down, like the gentle stretching that comes after active exercise. This is your time to breathe, to wander, to mull, and to dwell in the aftermath of concentrated writing practice. If you wish, choose one of the prayer forms from your faith tradition to close your writing session, or you may want to spend some time in wordless prayer. If you feel moved to do so, share your new awareness with your spiritual group, your spiritual director, or with a friend.

Writing can stir up feelings we thought were already processed and dealt with, or bring to light new perspectives that challenge us in their immediacy. If you feel troubled by the feelings or images that arose during the writing exercises, take a few minutes to write about what specifically triggered this response, if you can. Again, sharing your concerns or what you are noticing with your spiritual director, spiritual community, or with a trusted friend can help reduce or alleviate any tension or unease, especially if offered and received in a prayerful context.

## Thoughts on Doing Justice to Each Chapter

Each chapter in this book serves as an entryway into the topic at hand. Although the various steps ask challenging questions of you and offer thought-provoking writing exercises, most of these chapters could be the subject of a whole book. My intention is to help you develop the practice of writing within a prayerful context, as you begin to explore who you are in relationship with God. If any of these topics draw you toward further exploration, consider going back and approaching the topic again after a short break of a few days, to see what new wisdom and insights might arise. It may also be fruitful to bring these writings and new insights to another person: your spiritual director, pastoral counselor, trusted friend, or trusted community. Sharing what we write with someone we trust usually adds another layer of meaning and awareness.

PART II

*Beginning the Journey*

*S*ince I had found that the Divine had directed me out of a dead-end
street through my dreams, I thought that listening to God in a sleep-
less night might well be worth a try. The following night when I awoke, I got
up and went to a place where I could be warm. With journal and pencil in
hand, I spoke inwardly: "Well, God, here I am, what do you have on your
mind?" To my utter amazement, something spoke back to me. I recorded both
the questions and the answers. A real conversation followed, and these con-
versations have continued many nights during the past forty years.

—Morton Kelsey, *Set Your Hearts on the Greatest
Gift: Living the Art of Christian Love*

—Section 1—
# *Reading the Map*

*As I understand the gift of the spirit in art, so I understand prayer, and there is very little difference for me between prayer and writing. At their best, both become completely unselfconscious activities; the self-conscious, fragmented person is totally thrown away and integrated in work, and for the moments of such work, be it prayer or writing, I know wholeness, and sunside and nightside are no longer divided.*
>            —Madeleine L'Engle, *Madeleine L'Engle Herself:*
>                          *Reflections on a Writing Life*

Reading the map begins with locating the sign that says, "You are Here." In this section we focus on the person you are now. The viewpoint in these writing exercises is from where you stand, anchored in the present, taking stock of your own spiritual identity. Feel free to explore every corner of your personal self, including feelings, images, desires, attractions, and secret hopes.

# CHAPTER 1
## Images of My Spiritual Self

On the last day of my spiritual direction training program, we gathered together in a circle to "show and tell." Each of us had brought an image or an icon that represented how we saw ourselves as spiritual directors, as we imagined going forward into our new vocation. One woman brought a puppet shaped like a turtle: it represented both the interior and exterior life. A man brought a photograph of an important mentor/teacher. I brought a doll-sized chair, which I had painted and decorated with small charms. This chair represented my listening self. No icon, words, or pictures can capture all of our identity, but they can begin to tell a story, to highlight an important aspect of who we are, and who we want to be.

When asked to draw an image of your spiritual self, what would you draw? When asked to describe your spiritual self in words, what would you say? Images may come to mind that are suffused with color and texture. A memory of kneeling in church, or hiking though the woods, or sitting with a dying loved one may fill our minds and open our hearts. These experiences of spirit that infuse one's spiritual identity may or may not be related to the practice of religion, for our spiritual identity is partly composed of, yet much more than, our faith tradition, just as God is part of, yet much more than, any religious practice. Our spiritual identity is as unique as any other part of us, from our fingerprints to our way of living in the world. How would you describe the unique spirit that is you?

### Reflection

Because this is a book on writing as a spiritual practice, these exercises ask you to describe yourself today in words, rather than other mediums.

Begin to think about the images that spring to mind when you talk or write or think about who you are as a spiritual person.

- Do you picture yourself in a specific setting?
- Which emotions, rituals, or states of mind do you associate with your spiritual self?
- How does thinking about who you are, and how you are spiritually, summon up a particular attitude or framework for approaching your daily life?
- From there, begin to explore the feelings and assumptions attached to these images and states of mind or being. What are the emotions that color who you are spiritually?
- How do your usual thoughts or feelings about yourself change when you focus on who you are spiritually?

## Pen in Hand

Take some time to sketch in words or phrases, the images and descriptions that come to mind when you think about your spiritual self. These may be states of being such as grateful, obedient, restless; they may include descriptions like fluid, wellspring, open, seeking; or they may be emotions like fearful, eager, grateful. Write as many of these words and phrases down on a page as you can.

Don't worry about order or structure. Try to keep going past where you think you should or must stop—beyond the point where you think you are "done." See what arises. Sometimes the most honest and startling answers show up when we push a bit past our own limits.

## Noticing

- How did it feel to write this list?
- Which words or phrases were more interesting to you than others?
- Which words or images, if any, were disconcerting?
- Think about or write about how you feel now, after doing this exercise.

## On the Path

If a starting point or a direction has emerged from your list of words and images, use it as a way into this next exercise. Using that starting point, write more thoroughly about your spiritual self for fifteen minutes. If you find that you have said all that you can say before the time is up, try to write a little more. If you then feel that you have reached a final stopping point and your fifteen minutes aren't up, then write about the process itself until the time is up.

If you don't sense a natural starting point or direction, try using the suggested launching points below. Choose any that apply, or simply begin wherever you feel most drawn to begin.

- Describe the difference between your "daily self" and your spiritual self. If you don't feel there is any difference, write about how that came to be: was it always so? How did the integration of your daily self and spiritual self evolve?

Are there words or phrases that describe your spiritual self that you would not wish to share with others? With people in your faith community? What are they, and why? Do they seem subversive, or just different? Do they leave you feeling vulnerable? How would claiming these aspects of your spiritual identity feel?

- If the process of articulating your spiritual self was difficult, write about why that might be the case. How did it feel to struggle with this exercise?

## Contemplation

Finally, if you'd like to, re-read the section on contemplation on page 5 for some thoughts on how to conclude this chapter. Pay attention to how you feel now.

- Has the image of your spiritual self changed, expanded, or become more grounded? If not, what has happened?
- How will you take this new awareness into your life from this point?
- Do you feel like sharing what you wrote? Why? Why not?

# CHAPTER 2
## How Others Have Influenced My Spiritual Identity and My Relationship with God

A small girl watches carefully as her mother lights a candle, and eventually is allowed to light the candle by herself. A boy repeats the prayer he has been taught, learning the inflections before grasping the meaning. These actions become part of a child's spiritual vocabulary, part of who they are: actions that, while automatic, may or may not be heartfelt.

Who we are, in all aspects, is who we bring to God. Along the way to becoming who we are, the parents, religious leaders, lovers, relatives, and friends we have known have all at one point or another affected the way we view ourselves. Those relationships affect who we are in relation to God, even if indirectly. Like being draped in many-colored shawls, the influences of others can either be comforting and warm or too tightly binding with their constraints. In this chapter we will begin to unwind some of these cloths that the spirit is wrapped in, keeping those that bring color, warmth, and succor, and discarding those that weigh down and restrict spiritual freedom.

### Reflection

Begin to think about the influences that you've absorbed throughout life that impact your image of yourself as a spiritual person who has a relationship with God.

- Who are the people who have had the most impact on your spiritual identity?

- What words might others use to describe who you are and what your relationship to God is like?
- How important to you are other people's ideas or opinions about who you are as a spiritual person, or as a person in general?
- Which beliefs about yourself as someone who is, or can be, in relationship with God come from someone else?

## Pen in Hand

Spend a few minutes writing a mini-biography of yourself, from the point of view of someone else who has had a significant impact on your spiritual identity. Don't worry about formal writing. Treat this like a journal entry more than a letter of recommendation or character assessment. If you choose someone who you believe views you negatively, pay attention to any feelings of discomfort, anger, or anxiety that arise. Try to balance this portrait of yourself by writing another sketch, this time from the perspective of someone who has had a positive influence on you, who you believe cares for you.

## Noticing

- How did it feel to write a self-portrait from someone else's perspective?
- Was it difficult to think of someone who affirms you? Why is that?
- If you chose to write about someone who you believe judges you negatively, what insights did you gain about how her negative energy affects your spiritual identity?
- Think or write about the power of other people's influence on your own spiritual identity.

## On the Path

Writing about how others have influenced, shaped, or otherwise affected us can be either heartening or distressing, or sometimes a bit of both. For this next writing exercise, write about a single, significant person or interaction from your life that you continue to carry as part of your spiritual identity. Try to stay with this one person or experience that carries a lasting impression, in order to better explore its effect on you in more depth. There are often great riches to be explored in such a relationship, for if it has stayed with you, it must contain something important to explore. You can always repeat this exercise using a different focus another time.

It's natural to feel vulnerable opening ourselves up to outside influences, even if those influences have been positive. Ask God to accompany and safeguard you as you explore these imprints on your spirit. If nothing comes to you, some suggestions for getting started follow. Write for fifteen minutes.

- When did this person first begin to have an impact on your spiritual identity? What was it about this person that helped form you?
- If you could write to this person about their impact on your spiritual identity, what would you say?
- Do you feel mostly blessed by the people and events that have impacted you spiritually and affected your relationship with God, or do you feel that they have been a hindrance, that their influence has been detrimental or even damaging? Can you articulate why that is?
- What emotions arose through doing this exercise? Were there any surprises?

## Contemplation

Please bear in mind that you may be plumbing difficult emotional depths in this exercise. Anger, grief, or sadness aren't unusual responses. You may have stepped outside of yourself in order to reflect back on your experience through another's perspective, and that can be unsettling. Take some extra time to pray, share feelings, and experiences with a friend, or to nurture yourself. Think or write about:

- Was doing this exercise beneficial? In what way?
- Do you want to keep going with this exercise? Why? Why not?
- Has this exercise changed the way you view the people in your life?

# CHAPTER 3
## My Own Perspective on My Spiritual Identity and My Relationship to God

Underneath the labels, stereotypes, and opinions others hold about us exists our own private set of beliefs about who we are and what our relationship with God is all about. Someone may think "oh, she's so pious; she goes to church every week" while we secretly think of ourselves as rebellious outsiders who argue with God constantly. Or someone may see us as casual and indifferent spiritually, while inside, we long with all our hearts for God. When we articulate what we believe about ourselves, we begin to discover who we actually are. That makes it possible to grow into a fuller understanding of our true identity, and leads to acceptance, integration, and even transformation.

### Reflection

Begin to consider the ways you think about and express who you are as a spiritual person who has a relationship with God.

- What words or phrases best describe your spiritual identity?
- How comfortable are you with your spiritual identity?
- How does your spiritual identity help you connect with God?
- Are you living out the spiritual path you most desire?
- What images or symbols best describe your spiritual self?

### Pen in Hand

Spend a few minutes writing a mini-portrait of your spiritual self, this time from your own point of view. Again, don't worry about formal writing. Treat this like a journal entry more than a resume. Focus on describing what you visualize or feel when you say to yourself, "My spiritual identity is . . ."

## Noticing

- Is the way you imagine yourself more connected to images or words?
- When you picture your spiritual self, what are you doing? For instance, are you praying? With others? In nature?
- Can you separate who you are from what other people think about you? Would you like to?
- Is your own belief about your spiritual identity mostly positive, or mostly negative? How do you feel about that?

## On the Path

As you write, describe in more detail who you are as a spiritual person. Focus on how you come into connection with God. Write for fifteen minutes. If you'd like a way to begin, consider:

- In what settings are you most at home, most in touch with God?
- What does your spiritual practice look like? The rhythms, the rituals?
- How do you honor/nurture your spiritual self?
- Describe how your spiritual self is or is not congruent with your public persona.

## Contemplation

Spending time focused on and in relationship with our own self can bring us surprising and interesting information about ourselves. Honor your desire to get to know yourself and who you are in relationship with God. Think or write about:

- How are you feeling about yourself now?
- Do you have a clearer understanding of who you are in relation to God, or would you like to keep exploring that identity?
- Are you surprised at how easy or difficult it was to write a self-portrait? Why do you suppose that is?

# CHAPTER 4
## Beginning to Create
## My Spiritual Identity Anew

What avenues of creativity will you pursue on your spiritual journey? How will you create the way you live in the world from this moment on? One of the most precious gifts from God is the freedom to create. It is not just artists who create, with words and paint and music: all human beings are free to create a self, an approach to life, a way of being in the world. Being from God, this creative freedom is imbued with God's presence, so that while we are free to turn away from God, we are also free to embrace God's presence as co-creator in the continually evolving creation that is our life. Consciously choosing to co-create our spiritual self with God, new possibilities open up for greater freedom, authenticity, and joy.

## Reflection

Begin to think about how you would like to co-create your spiritual self in the newness of this moment, this point on your life journey.

- How do you feel when thinking about "cocreating your spiritual self?"
- What feelings arise in you at the thought of change?
- What about your spiritual self do you want to keep?
- Which aspects of your spiritual self, if any, do you want to reclaim from your past?
- What would you like to discard?

## Pen in Hand

Write about what it means to you to partner with God in creating your spiritual self. Are you comfortable with that concept? Why or why not? Which aspects of your spiritual identity or spiritual practice would you like to reconsider and make anew?

## Noticing

- What was it like to write from this perspective?
- Did you experience more or less resistance to this exercise compared to other topics you have written about? Why?
- What did you learn in doing this exercise?
- Were you affirmed in any way during this exercise?

## On the Path

Our spiritual selves are always evolving. But paying attention to that fact and actively participating in our evolution or re-creation isn't easy. This exercise, however, invites you to spend that time, and participate, even if it is difficult. Spend fifteen minutes or more, writing about your role as co-creator of your life. Part of creating is pushing the limits a bit, stretching to meet God. Reflect on some of the questions listed here if you feel stuck.

- How does the concept of creative freedom fit into your spirituality?
- Where do you feel God acting creatively in your life?
- Where do you notice resistance to God or to creative change? What does that resistance look like?
- Where has your creativity been allowed free expression in your spiritual life?

## Contemplation

Acknowledging the possibility of cocreating ourselves anew can feel disturbing or intimidating, or it can be a welcome challenge. It can also be all of these things at once. Yet this invitation to create your spiritual identity anew is not mandatory; it is a choice, stemming from our free choice to be in relationship with God.

- What feelings arose in you most strongly, most insistently during this exercise?
- What would it be like to share these feelings, either in conversation, through writing, or through some other form of expression?
- Do you want to explore this topic in more depth?

# —Section 2—
## *Using the Compass: My Religious Tradition and My Relationship with God*

*In the beginning was the word . . . with its roots simultaneously in the Hebrew and the Greek tradition—in the Hebrew tradition, where the very first act of God in the first chapter of the first book of the Bible is to speak, and in the Greek tradition, where the word for "word" and the word for "reason" are the same—this declaration affirms that the act of communication is at the very center not only of human existence and its origins but of the mystery of the Divine Being itself. And so the transmission of the word, the moving of the word from within to without, from the word that dwells within to the word that emerges . . . the mystery of that process is the mystery of divine communication and of divine self-communication, and therefore of the Divine Self.*
—Jaroslav Pelikan, "Writing as a Means of Grace" in *Spiritual Quests: The Art and Craft of Religious Writing*

A woman enters a place of worship and enacts a private ritual. A community gathers to celebrate a particular sacrament, a rite of passage, or to honor a time in its history with a song. Words are read from a sacred text, by someone chosen to read them.

What images came to mind when you read these sentences? Do these images express the meaning and the practical reality of your religious tradition? How do they coincide, or conflict with, your actual experience of God?

The way a particular religion portrays God may or may not coincide with the actual faith experience of someone who practices that religion. The elements of reason, historical tradition, and social and cultural influences all enter into the mix of what constitutes a religion, along with the experiences of faith and encounters with God that each person brings. In this section you are invited to explore in writing where our religion and our heart's knowing and longing intersect and diverge.

# CHAPTER 5
## Envisioning God

The image of God as a man with a long, flowing white beard has become a cliché in American culture. Nowadays the images we are exposed to may be more diverse, more creative, but are they our own? Most people grow up with some inherited image of God: an image absorbed from faith traditions, family, culture, and/or the media. The sacred texts of the various religious traditions are filled with a variety of diverse images, as are contemporary movies, music, ads, and other media. But how do we—each of us—image God for ourselves? What image or images speak most clearly for us? Do we have an image of God that is ours alone? Use the exercises in this section to begin exploring or discerning an image of God that helps draw you closer into relationship with the Holy One.

### Reflection

What would you say to someone who asks, "What (or who) is God?" Would your first response come in the form of words or as an image? Would your response be a physical one? Would you feel something, or imagine something, or recall a personal experience? Free yourself from all constraints put upon your imagination by religion. Think about who God is for you before any art, images, or words were given to you either by your religious tradition, your culture, or your family. Who is the God of your own experience? Have you ever had an experience of God that shapes your image or understanding?

## Pen in Hand

Write a description of God using metaphor, imagery, story, or any other form of writing. What color is God? What does God sound like? What does God feel like against your skin, in your body? What does God taste like, or smell like? Can you ground God in the senses? Or is God more ephemeral, located not here or there, but rather a state of mind or a way of being or feeling? Write down what you *know* from personal experience.

## Noticing

- What was it like to describe God from this perspective?
- Which responses surprised you?
- Did you notice any feelings as you wrote? What were they?
- How does it feel to focus so closely on your personal experience of God?

## On the Path

Write about the experience of writing, thinking, and feeling freely about God, rather than limiting yourself to an understanding inherited from other sources. What changes might you experience if you gave yourself this freedom more often? What might you do with this freedom? How might it affect your relationship with God? Are there any areas in your life where you feel particularly free? How might this freedom infuse your spiritual life? You may want to ask yourself:

- When have you felt the most free to be with God?
- How would it feel to create a new image of God?
- How do you feel about practicing freedom in your spiritual life?
- How does it feel to write about spiritual freedom?

## Contemplation

Did any self-critical or judgmental voices appear during this exercise? Did it feel frivolous or even blasphemous to envision God for yourself? Were you enjoying yourself, or feeling ill at ease? There are no right or wrong answers to these questions. Notice what went on in you when you were asked to create room for a new image of God, and to enter into the imagining and creating process. Bring these feelings to God if that's helpful.

- What is different now, after writing, in how you feel about your spiritual journey?
- How did this writing exercise change how you feel about God?
- Where might you want to go next with what you have learned about yourself?

# CHAPTER 6
## How My Religious Tradition Portrays God

What image of God dominates your worship setting and would most impact a visitor unfamiliar with this setting? What icon or words would you choose if you wanted to describe to someone from another tradition how your tradition portrays God? Writing about how our particular religious tradition portrays God can be a helpful exercise in understanding how aspects of our image of God have been absorbed and integrated over time through worship attendance, reading, messages from religious leaders, and other external sources. Even those who have not been raised in a particular faith tradition have most likely accumulated images, assumptions, descriptions, and even anecdotes about "who God is" according to various religions. What are these influences, and how do they impact the spiritual journey?

**Reflection**

What would you say to someone who asks, "Who is the God of your religious tradition?" (If you have not been so raised, but have been more influenced by one tradition than others, or are attracted by one more than others, then ask yourself the questions from the perspective of an interested observer. You may also have been raised in one religion and have now chosen another; choose which tradition you would most like to explore at this time.)

- Where does your first reaction to this question come from? Your heart? Your intellect? Someplace else?

25

- What feelings do you notice when you think about
  this question?
- What might the response be if were you to ask this question of
  others, about your own tradition? (i.e., "What does our faith
  believe about who God is and how God works?")
- What is important about this question for you at this point in
  time? Why?
- What meaning has this question held for you in the past? Why?

## Pen in Hand

Write a list of nouns or verbs that describe the God of your faith tradition. Focus on describing how God is portrayed rather than the doctrine or structure of your religion. Write down all of the attributes you
can think of, based directly on what you have been taught, what you
have read, or how you think the God of your tradition is portrayed in
your culture or within your religious institution. Include those attributes that you agree and disagree with.

## Noticing

- What was it like to describe God from this perspective?
- Did any of your responses surprise you?
- Did you notice any feelings attached to this description? What
  were they?
- How did you feel about focusing on your faith tradition's
  understanding rather than you own experience of God?

## On the Path

For fifteen minutes, write down everything you know about God as
portrayed by your religion. If you don't have enough information to
fill fifteen minutes, write about images portrayed in the media, and
impressions picked up along the way from friends, books, places of
worship you might have visited, and so on. If you still run out of things
to say, then write about that lack of information; what are the life

circumstances that lead to this lack of information? As you are writing, if you get stuck you might want to write about:

- Where does most of your information about the God of your religious tradition come from? (i.e., teachers, parents, books, media)
- Of these sources of information, which has had the most impact on you?
- What feelings do you have about these sources of information?
- How do you feel about learning more about your religion and how God is portrayed, both historically and currently?

## Contemplation

Thinking and writing more objectively about the religious tradition that has shaped our image of God can be both a welcome and sobering exercise. Spend some time reconnecting with your own personal knowledge of God, which both precedes and supersedes the knowledge we have acquired from outside sources.

- What differences do you notice now, after writing, in how you feel about your religious tradition?
- What differences do you notice now, after writing, in how you feel about God?
- What is stirring in you about your religious tradition: Curiosity? Disinterest?
- Where might you go next with this awareness?

# CHAPTER 7
## How My Religious Tradition Portrays Who I Am

Religion not only describes who God is, but also offers many definitions about who its members are. Some of these definitions might include, but are certainly not limited to: sheep in a fold; warriors for God; seekers and holders of truth, receivers of the Word; stewards of the earth; children; servants; Chosen; one as part of the Whole; unique yet interconnected with all. While spiritual identity is individual, religious identity is more corporate: what applies to one, applies to all (although distinctions are made in the various roles its members occupy, especially in religions with a clerical hierarchy). This chapter addresses the global identity that is assumed like a mantle for the members of a religious tradition. How comfortable we are with that mantle has much to do with how comfortable we are in faith community and in religious practice.

### Reflection

Think about what you would say to someone who asks, "How does your religion describe who you are?"

- What feelings are already present as you approach this topic?
- How do you feel about being described or identified by your religious tradition?
- Where does your understanding of your role come from?

- Before this exercise, how much had you thought about how your religion portrays you?
- Why do you think you have, or haven't, thought about it?

## Pen in Hand

Write a list of nouns or verbs that you think someone of your own religious tradition, in a similar role, might use to describe you. Describe from their point of view both who you are personally as a member of your faith community, and how you are perceived as a member of the larger community of your whole faith tradition. For instance, would they name things such as your gender, race, role, and participation in the community as significant descriptors? Would they use theological understandings to describe you? What other ways might someone describe you from within your faith tradition?

## Noticing

- How do you feel about writing about yourself from another perspective?
- What is it like to step outside of yourself in this way?
- Do you feel limited or freed by this description? Why?
- Are there words or images that you wished your faith tradition would use to describe you that aren't commonly used? What are they?

## On the Path

Write down everything you know or believe about how you, as an individual person of faith, might be portrayed by your faith tradition or community. Then write about how you, as a member of a specific class, race, gender, sexual orientation, political persuasion, and so on, might be described by your religious tradition. To more fully explore this topic as you are writing, you might want to explore:

- How might your religion separate who you are as a spiritual person from who you are as a member of several subsets of the

human race (i.e., your gender, your race, etc.) and how do you
feel about that?

- What are the historical versus the current religious attitudes
  toward who and what you are?
- How do you feel as you address this topic?
- What parts of what you are writing and feeling now are affected
  by what you have been taught as doctrine, as opposed to
  how you have actually been treated by members of your faith
  community, both in the past and currently?

## Contemplation

How important it is to our spirit to feel like a welcomed or honored
member of our faith. Writing about the value and respect our religious
tradition holds for its members can renew a sense of belonging. Yet
even if we struggle instead with feeling unequal or unwelcome within
our immediate faith community or the larger community of our religion, sharing our experience of membership in our religious tradition is
a positive and healing first step toward greater unity with God. Spend
some time contemplating whether it might benefit you to share these
experiences with another person, or a safe group of people, as you bring
who you are in spirit to the table of connection with others.

- How are feeling about what you just wrote?
- Do you need anything from God, and/or from someone you can
  trust? What is that? How might you ask for what you need?
- Would you like to say or write more about this topic? Why?
  Why not?

# CHAPTER 8
## What Attracts Me about My Religion?

A brightly colored bird flickers past the window. Music floats on the air in four-part harmony. A polished wood railing glides easily under the hand, warm to the touch. Attracted by the sights, sounds, and touch of life, we draw closer, our attention held by the invitation to joy. Attraction is the catalyst that stirs us to embrace life. Love is fed and sustained by attraction, including the love we feel for our religious tradition. By paying attention to what attracts us, we can uncover the delight, the spiritual power, the nourishment, and the regenerative aspects of our faith.

### Reflection

What images or memories come to mind when you think about what attracts you to your religion?

- What words, images, or actions appealed to you as you were growing up?
- What aspects of your religion continue to attract you?
- Is it difficult or easy to think about what continues to attract you? Write about why that may be so.
- How do you feel about focusing on your religion in this way?
- Is your attraction to your community a regular or occasional occurrence? Why is that so?

## Pen in Hand

Write down as many words as you can think of that describe your attraction to your religious tradition. Use colored pencils, crayons, markers, paints, or pastels if you have them. Draw any images that come to mind as well. Make your page as "attractive" as possible, not just by trying to make it pretty, but by using the colors, images, words, or symbols that you are most attracted to in your life. Try to fill the whole page.

## Noticing

- How did it feel to make something that you find appealing and that portrays how you feel about your religious tradition?
- Was it easy or difficult to come up with enough words or images to fill the page? Why?
- Are there particular colors or words that you didn't expect to use before you started? Where do you think the impetus to use them came from?
- How does it feel to have put your feelings into words and images?

## On the Path

Take fifteen minutes to turn those images and words into a short narrative on what it is about your religious tradition that first attracted you and what continues to attract you. Stay focused on the positive; we will spend time with the negative or upsetting in the next chapter. For now, practice staying with the topic of attraction. Discover or rediscover what it is about your religion that you first loved and continue to love. If you find it difficult to write enough about what attracts you for fifteen minutes, use the following prompts to keep going. Stay with it, and you may reach a new level of awareness.

- Describe your attraction to your faith tradition in terms of the worship service. What about the music, the rhythm of the service, the words, the visual imagery, and the setting appeals to you?

- Choose one memory of feeling deeply attracted and describe it in detail. What was happening at the time? Who was present? Describe the physical sensations that went along with the experience.
- Compare an experience of attraction within a religious setting or context to any similar experience outside of this context (i.e., at work, in a personal relationship, in nature). How are they similar?
- What do you do, or can you do, to foster and to nurture this dynamic experience of attraction?

## Contemplation

Just as love at first sight often becomes something deeper over time—something that may seem to lack passion on the surface but that sustains us more powerfully—so can our first flush of passion with our faith tradition fade over time. Remembering from time to time why we came to our religious life or community helps nourish that ember so the fire can continue to warm our souls. Spend some time in contemplation reveling in those experiences of attraction and desire, and seek ways in which you can nurture them regularly.

- What feelings have arisen that need expression?
- What might you say to God about the attraction you have to your religious tradition?
- How can you continue to recognize and engage with what attracts you?

# CHAPTER 9
## What Do I Find Repelling about My Religion?

Feeling repelled is a more intense reaction than feeling bothered. In this context "repelled" doesn't mean being disgusted, but feeling "pushed against" or pushed away. Being repelled by something or someone implies a strong energy force moving against us, propelling us away from where we want to be, despite our attempts otherwise. Receptivity gets shut down, and it is easy to stop thinking, noticing, and experiencing the presence of God within a religious setting. Sometimes that's experienced in a passive way, as being repelled by forces outside us against our wishes: "We don't want you here." Sometimes we experience this in more active ways, such as choosing to disagree with or disapprove of various aspects of our tradition: "I can't go along with that teaching." Responses to feeling repelled include anything from participating by rote as members of a faith community, to avoiding religious practice and community altogether. By writing about what repels us, we can more clearly recognize, articulate, and even transform our own attitudes toward our religious tradition. From there, we are free either to accept or change what prevents us from more fully being with God.

### Reflection

What images, experiences, or words come to mind when you reflect on what repels you in your religious tradition?

- Does thinking about this topic make you uncomfortable? If so, what disturbs you? What aspects of your tradition have always repelled you?

- What aspects of your tradition newly or more recently repel you?
- Where does your feeling emanate from? From within?
  From without?
- How much is this feeling impacting your relationship with God?

## Pen in Hand

Make a list of as many synonyms (words that mean the same) as you can for the word "repelled." Feel free to mix tenses and to stretch for words that don't have the same exact meaning but fall within the same range. Then write down as many antonyms (words that mean the opposite) as you can for the word "repel." Write as many synonyms and antonyms as you can.

## Noticing

- What do you notice about the two lists?
- Was it harder to come up with synonyms or antonyms?
- What are the differences in feeling generated by these two lists?
- Are there particular words that you didn't expect to use before you started?
- How does it feel to have put your feelings into words?

## On the Path

Now that you have a page with words and images, take fifteen minutes to turn those images and words into a short narrative on what it is about your religious tradition that you find bothersome, repelling, or would like to change. While this topic can evoke many upsetting feelings, try to balance out the emotions that may come pouring out by staying within the format of narrative. While simply "dumping" feelings onto the page can be liberating for the moment, the process of clearly articulating strong emotion in a more objective, narrative way can be transformative for the long term.

- Describe what repels you about your faith tradition in terms of the worship service. What about the music, the rhythm of

the service, the words, the visual imagery, the rituals, and the
sanctuary prevents you from opening to God?

- Recall a time when you felt deeply repelled from God and
describe it in detail. What were the circumstances? Feelings?
Was the situation resolved?

- Compare an experience of feeling repelled within a religious
setting or context to any similar experience outside of this
context (i.e., at work, in a personal relationship, in nature).
How are they similar?

- What can you do to shift this energy, either in terms of your
outlook or your own immediate situation within your personal
or community relationships?

## Contemplation

By acknowledging and confronting the darker aspects of our feelings
about our faith tradition, a door opens into new possibilities. We may
begin to understand how negative experiences have played a part in
distancing ourselves from God. What we do with this information is
part of the continuing discernment of the spiritual path.

- Do you need to process further the feelings that have arisen from
this exercise? How might you do that in a safe and healing way?

- What might you say to God about the distance between you?

- How can you continue to recognize and confront what
repels you?

# CHAPTER 10
## Exploring My Relationship
## to My Faith Community

As you write your responses to the exercises in this book, you are engaging in a solitary act; you are engaged with God but not with other people. After writing, people often want to share what they have written, as a way of being with God *and* with other people. Writers (and if you are writing responses to these exercises, then you are a writer) seek out a community when they can, as a way to alleviate isolation, and as a means of extending and transforming the spiritual practice of writing from a solitary act to a communal sharing and exchange. Community is part of participating in the writing tradition.

Full participation in a religious tradition also includes commitment to a faith community, which usually involves: people in pastoral leadership positions of one form or another; a gathering of members; a shared mission; a shared vision; and a belief in the importance and sacredness of connection with others. As with writing, faith community is a way to alleviate isolation, and a way to extend and transform personal spiritual practice into a communal sharing and exchange. How we feel about the religious community to which we have dedicated our spiritual selves impacts our relationship with God. The role we hold within the community can also either facilitate or impede our experience of God.

### Reflection

Close your eyes and visualize a gathering of your faith community. Imagine yourself in worship with the group. Also imagine yourself in a

sacred setting such as a wedding, funeral, or baptism. Then visualize a social gathering of this same community doing something you are familiar
with like a fundraiser, coffee hour after services, or a picnic. Pay attention
to where you are and what you are doing in these various settings.

- In which setting are you most comfortable?
- Who are the people around you? How do you feel about them?
  Why?
- What role do you play in your community?
- How do you feel about that role?

## Pen in Hand

In this exercise we will examine the relationship between ourselves and
our community. (If you are not currently a member of a community,
then use a community from your past as a model, or one you are
considering joining, or one you would like to create.) I'd like you to
draw a family tree that encompasses everyone in your faith community,
labeling everyone by name, or role, or general position in the community (i.e., pastoral leader, lay leaders, general congregation, etc.). You
can approach this several ways. You can put the designated leader at the
top and work down from there in a hierarchical framework (you could
also put a religious figure at the very top of the tree, depending on your
tradition). You may prefer to draw a mandala and arrange everyone in
layers within the circle. You may prefer concentric circles, or a pyramid
shape. Or you may prefer to draw a map, or a blueprint of your
worship setting, placing everyone in their designated spots. The goal is
to lay out in visual form, the pattern of power, relationship, and interconnectedness within your faith community.

## Noticing

- Was it easy or difficult to think of a model for your community?
- How does the model of your community match, or deviate from,
  the model of the larger denomination?
- How do you feel about where you are on the map, tree,
  blueprint, or mandala?

- What do you notice now, looking at your completed work, that you hadn't thought about before?

## On the Path

Write a narrative describing your relationship to your faith community. Start with the model you created in the last exercise, but flesh it out by articulating how you feel about each aspect of this model. Write about how this model impacts your ability to connect with God, either in a positive or negative way (often it's both). Here are some reflections to consider as you write. You may find yourself needing more than fifteen minutes!

(Again, if you are not currently a member of a faith community, then feel free to write about a faith community from your past. Or, you may describe an ideal community you'd like to join or create.)

- Describe how you would change the way your community is designed, or what you would not change about your faith community.
- Describe which role you might like to have, or one you wish you didn't currently have.
- Describe your relationship to your faith leader(s). How is your relationship facilitated or impeded by their presence, leadership, and actions?
- What would you like to say to God about your faith community?

## Contemplation

Thinking and writing about our community and the part we play in it can bring to light important aspects of our relationship with God, which we might otherwise tend to think of as taking place only within ourselves. It helps us widen our perspective, as we begin to notice the larger context in which we nourish and express that relationship. We begin to see what our community does or does not offer us, as well as what we can or cannot contribute, either by virtue of our own personality, our comfort level, how welcome we feel, or the conditions placed upon our ability to participate by the larger community and denomination.

- How might you continue to explore who you are in relation to your faith community?
- Can you share your feelings with someone within your community?
- Where do you find God within your faith community experiences?
- What might have changed for you by doing these exercises?

# Section 3
## *Milestones on the Path*

*Push yourself beyond when you think you are done with what you have to say. Go a little further. Sometimes when you think you are done, it is just the edge of beginning. Probably that's why we decide we are done. It's getting too scary. We are touching down into something real. It is beyond the point when you think you are done that something strong comes out.*
—Natalie Goldberg, *Writing Down the Bones*

The stages of life—childhood, adolescence, and so on—offer rich glimpses into the settings, emotions, people, and events that have shaped our spirituality. The crucial crossroads and turning points taken together tell the graced, vital, and precious story of your life journey toward a closer relationship with God.

# CHAPTER 11
## Childhood

Over the years, in workshops and writing exercises, I have been asked to recall a moment from childhood when I felt the presence of God. I always return to a memory of standing in my father's vegetable garden, next to the tomato plants. I am about six years old, and he has offered to pay me a penny for each tomato slug that I can find and pick off the plants. I can still feel the hot sun on my skin and see the soft, green, squishy slugs in my fingers. I can smell the tomatoes and I hear bees humming nearby. I am happy. I don't know why this memory is the one that comes to mind: I don't remember thinking about, or even knowing about God then. But it returns; persistent, heightened against other blurred memories; precious to me.

Childhood may be a fairly recent memory or a distant one in terms of chronology; in terms of its continuing impact, the years fall away. Most of us carry the little girl or little boy we once were in physical form in our memories, sensory experiences, and the gifts and the wounds brought forward from that time. You may or may not have felt as though you knew God's presence as a child. In either case, ask God to be present to you now as you seek God in the child you once were, the child who is a precious part of the person you are now.

### Reflection

Spend some time remembering your childhood. Using your imagination, place yourself in the past. Stay with the images that are most pleasing, most comforting. We will explore grief, anger, and fear issues later in the book; for now, although your childhood may have been fraught with these things, try to stay with the positive memories of being a child. If that is not possible for you at this time, you may want to spend some time on the Section Four themes first, and return to this exercise later.

Imagine yourself in a favorite childhood place where you felt safe and happy. Notice the colors of this place. Feel the temperature. Notice what you are wearing and what objects are in this place. Pay attention to how your body feels, what sounds you hear, and what time of day it is. Let yourself re-experience this place and the way it makes you feel. Stay with this feeling and the images for as long as you want to.

- Was it difficult to recall a favorite childhood place? If so, what made it difficult?
- What feelings does remembering this place evoke?
- How connected do you feel to your childhood?
- How are you connected to the child you once were?
- How might God have been present in this memory?

### Pen in Hand

Childhood is a wild garden that we could wander in for a very long time. For now, center your attention on a small portion of that garden. Choose a particular place, event, or activity from your childhood that evoked feelings of joy, comfort, fun, and wonder. For now, try to stay with one memory, or a series of memories that are all linked by this particular place, event, or activity. As you write, describe this place, event, or activity. Write about the colors, the sounds, the feel of things—the sensory aspects you remember and treasure. Describe this memory as if you are writing to someone who has no knowledge whatsoever of that experience. You are writing to the spirit and writing from your child self, to your adult self: a reminder of something you may have long forgotten, but can now reclaim as part of your graced history. Feel free to repeat this exercise again later, using a new memory as your focus.

## Noticing

- How do you feel after writing about this experience?
- Does this experience remind you of any aspect of your current life?
- Is your experience or image of God consistent with any aspect of this experience? How?
- What might you reclaim from this part of your childhood that could help you in your spiritual journey?

## On the Path

Choose a memory of an experience of God's presence from your childhood; don't use the same one you just wrote about. If you can't remember a time when you consciously felt close to God, try to think of a time that you now know, in retrospect, was an experience of God. Was there a time when you were aware of a presence, of something larger than yourself, or a time when you sensed that you were connected to the wider continuum and movement of life? Perhaps your sense of God's presence was characterized by a feeling of great joy and wonder, comfort, of compassion, or deep and abiding love, whether through or apart from a human relationship. Write about this memory. Describe the details that make the memory come alive for you. Include something about the setting, your feelings, and the sensory details. Before you begin and as you write, invite God to be in this memory with you now, as God was then. If you need ways to re-enter this childhood garden, try answering these questions for yourself as you write:

- Describe how this experience came upon you: was it sudden, unexpected, or was it an experience that happened often?
- If you are just now finding God in this childhood experience, describe how that feels. What emotions are stirring in you as you reclaim this experience as an experience of God?
- How private is this memory for you? Why?
- If you have continued to revisit this memory throughout your life, why is that so? If you have not revisited this memory before, why do you think that's the case?

## Contemplation

Revisiting our childhood, we enter a whole world of both darkness and light, as seasons come and go and we learn to find our way again. We recognize the child who struggled and danced, cried and laughed. When we look for glimpses of God in those moments, we are often rewarded with the joy, comfort, and wonder we may have lost sight of along the way. For God was there, and as we discover or rediscover that awareness, we may meet God again, as we did for the first time. If you feel the need to process the emotions that arose during this writing, seek someone out that you feel safe with, and talk with them. You may also want to pray, telling God how you feel.

- How have your feelings toward your childhood (and the child you were) been changed by the writing you have done?
- Have your feelings toward God changed in the light of this awareness?
- Would you like to share memories and feelings about the child you were with someone else?
- What might the child in you say to God or ask of God?

# Chapter 12
## Adolescence

A youth minister once told me how much he liked working with teenagers. "It's like I'm right back there, in adolescence," he said, smiling. He couldn't understand why more people didn't want to work with teenagers; he felt real joy in their presence. "Precisely because it takes them right back there, to adolescence," I suggested. Not everyone wants to go back there, but he had found real gifts in that stage of life, both the first time around, and now as an adult.

If childhood was a garden for most of us, at least at times, then surely adolescence was a wilderness. Adolescence is a time of rapid changes. We moved from dependent to independent, from graceful to awkward and back again, sometimes daily. We may have felt great, indefinable longing: would we ever discover what we are here for, who we are? Some teens needed long stretches of solitude: time alone in the wilderness, communing with ourselves and God. Others needed the company of others, particularly of those who seemed to know the way. For still others, God's presence wasn't obvious in this midst of those changes, but God was there, and God's presence may be found in looking backward.

### Reflection

Spend some time remembering your adolescence. Place yourself in the past, in your imagination. Allow yourself to feel again the powerful forces that seemed to sweep through your body, thoughts, and emotions, as you sought your footing and tried to establish your place on holy ground.

46

Imagine yourself in a situation when you felt most truly integrated, free, and full of glory, as an adolescent. You may have been discovering true friendship for the first time, or practicing a new skill, or a new art form. You may have been dancing, or playing a sport, or simply discovering the world with new, awakened eyes. You may have discovered some new talent of yours, some gift or even something that was just incredibly fun, like riding roller coasters. Imagine, think, and feel your way into this teenager that you once were. Where are you? What are you wearing? How old are you? What has caused you to feel so happy, so empowered, so alive? Even if this memory is fleeting, take some moments now to revisit it, to savor it.

We will explore grief, anger, and fear issues later in the book: for now, although your childhood may have been fraught with these things, try to stay with the positive memories of being a teenager. If that is not possible for you at this time, you may want to spend some time with the Recognizing and Navigating the Landscape themes first, and return to this section later.

- Was it difficult to remember feeling free and empowered?
- What feelings does remembering yourself as a teenager evoke?
- How connected do you feel to your adolescence?
- How are you connected to the teenager you once were?
- How might God have been present in this memory?

## Pen in Hand

If children are the innocents in our spiritual kingdom, then teenagers are the poor. Teenagers feel cast out of one reality and are still finding their way toward another. In a spiritual sense they are adrift, homeless, searching for the form and function their lives will take, eager to get going, but with no place yet to go. They have lost or cast away many of the accoutrements of childhood, including unselfconscious grace, naiveté, and wonder, and yet they are not yet encumbered with the material, physical, or spiritual baggage of adulthood. Wandering in this seemingly empty state, God can be easily overlooked in the confusion, passions, and distractions of daily life. Where did you meet God in adolescence?

Set aside fifteen minutes to write about a time as a teenager when you felt most completely in harmony with yourself and your life. Choose a moment in time when you were able to incorporate all of the disparate aspects of your identity, in full glory and freedom. You may choose to expand on the image you thought of in the reflection or choose another moment. Feel free to repeat this exercise again later, using a new memory as your focus.

## Noticing

- How do you feel after writing about this experience?
- Does this experience remind you of any aspect of your current life?
- Does your current experience or image of God fit with any aspect of this prior experience? How?
- What might you reclaim from this part of your adolescence that could help you in your spiritual journey?

## On the Path

The process you used for uncovering the presence of God in childhood can also be effective in exploring adolescence. In choosing a memory of God's presence, pay attention both to your body then and your body now, as you write. Our sexuality (explored in more detail in chapter 24) plays a large part in our overall awakening to life and to God. If you wish to focus on a moment in your sexual or sensual experience, feel free to choose that. If your memories simply include a feeling of body awareness, feel free to explore that here as well.

If you find yourself unable to remember a time in adolescence when you consciously felt close to God, try to think of a time that you now know, in retrospect, was an experience of God. As with childhood experiences, this may be characterized by an awareness of a presence, of something larger than yourself, or a sense of yourself in relation to a wider continuum and movement of life. It may also be characterized by a feeling of great joy and wonder, comfort, or compassion. If you find you are drawn to explore a memory of falling in love, or discovering a passion of some kind, write about this memory. Describe the details that make the memory come alive for you. Include something about the setting, your feelings, and the sensory details, but keep the focus on yourself. Spend a few moments before you begin, inviting God to be in this memory with you now, as God was then. If you need ways to re-enter this adolescent wilderness, try answering these questions for yourself as you write:

- Describe this experience that affected you so powerfully that you still remember and feel its intensity. What about it affects you so strongly?
- If you are just now finding God in this moment from adolescence, describe how that feels. What emotions are stirring in you as you reclaim this memory as an experience of God?
- How private is this memory for you? Why?
- If you have continued to revisit this memory throughout your life, why is that? If you have not revisited this memory before, why is that?

## Contemplation

Revisiting our adolescence can remind us of a stage of life that we loved and hated, often at the same time. Asking God to accompany us to that wilderness time gives us the opportunity to stand with and embrace the teenager we once were, this time with the wisdom and compassion of adulthood. As in childhood, we cannot redo the past, or unmake any mistakes, but we can reclaim an awareness of God in those memories. We can rediscover the wondrous courage, tenacity, and capacity for love that we carried with us, whether we were conscious of it or not at the time, for we are conscious of it now, with God's love. If you feel the need to process the emotions that arose during this writing, seek someone out that you feel safe with, and talk with them. You may also want to pray, telling God how you feel.

- How have your feelings toward your adolescence (and the teenager you were) changed as a result of the writing you have done?
- Have your feelings toward God changed in the light of this awareness?
- What would you like to reclaim of your adolescent self?
- What might you say to God or ask of God about your adolescence?

# CHAPTER 13
## Young Adulthood

A diploma on the wall. A checking account. A car. Signing a lease on an apartment. Young adults often mark progress by external accomplishments. Leaving home, going to college, finding a job or career, and for some marrying and having children are a few of the signposts along the way of young adulthood. For many, these are busy years, ones where building the foundations of adult life occupy much of our time. The flurry of activities may lead us to God, or prevent us from taking the time to notice God's presence. Whether you are in the midst of this stage of life or are reflecting back on our young adult years, you can look for God's presence in the midst of the choices, disappointments, discoveries, and mistakes.

### Reflection

Think about yourself as a young adult. Imagine yourself in a familiar setting: school, or work, or in your household. What are you wearing? What do you spend most of your time doing? What is the predominant concern that you have? What is the predominant emotion? In your thoughts, do you live mostly in the past, the present, or the future? How do you feel about your body? What are you most hoping for, in the immediate future? Introduce yourself or reacquaint yourself with this person from the inside out.

- How do you feel toward this young adult that is you?
- What are your hopes and dreams?
- What do you most fear?

- Where are you putting most of your energy?
- What are your experiences of God?

## Pen in Hand

In young adulthood we grapple with the expectations placed on us by ourselves, our culture, and by our families. We take on responsibility for ourselves and reject the demands placed on us as children and teenagers, often including the assumption that we will attend religious services regularly. No one watches over us anymore, and for better or worse, we are on our own. Are we also on our own from God? We can discern God's continuing presence in our young adult lives by examining more closely the challenges that confront us.

Set aside fifteen minutes to write about a decision you made or need to make as a young adult. Choose a decision that particularly pertains to the circumstances of young adulthood: one involving a career, educational, or workplace issue, a significant relationship issue, or one involving where you will live. Let your feelings be your guide in choosing which one to write about. Write about the circumstances surrounding this decision in order to "set the scene," but then focus more closely on how you feel/felt about this decision. Feel free to repeat this exercise again later, using a new decision as your focus.

## Noticing

- How do you feel about having to make this decision?
- If you have already made it, how does it feel to revisit it?
- How do you now feel about the outcome?
- What drew you to choose this particular decision to explore?

## On the Path

In young adulthood we make decisions on a daily basis that we may or may not feel prepared for. We want to be and to feel independent and unencumbered by the need to ask for help from our parents. Seeking out the advice and companionship of peers may provide comfort and reassurance, a feeling of "we are all in this together." Yet ultimately we are responsible only to ourselves, as we make momentous decisions that may impact the course of our lives: who will we love, how will we live, what work will we do?

God is the current running through all of these life choices, whether we are (or were) conscious of that at this point in our lives, or not. No longer "forced" to participate in a religious tradition, many of us opt for what feels like freedom from dogma, doctrine, and boredom. Yet with that freedom comes a new responsibility, also given us by the spirit: to choose how we will forge our relationship with God.

If you are a young adult, explore a decision that faces you right now. How will you choose, which way will you go? Ask God in prayer to be with you as you write about this decision.

If you are writing about your young adulthood by looking into the past, choose a decisive moment that still resonates with you today. Write about where you now see God in the decision you made and the process you went through to make it.

Write until you feel some sense of resolution, or clarification, or a shift in your perspective. List the practical aspects of your decision, such as money, time concerns, and so on, as well as emotional reactions and spiritual concerns. Write as if you are consulting with a wise elder who is nonjudgmental, has no agenda about the outcome, and wants the best for you. Here are some guidelines if you need them:

- Is there something you are waiting for, that you need in order to make this decision? What is it?
- What practical resources have you used or will you use to make this decision?
- What spiritual resources have you used or will you use to make this decision?
- Where is God in this decision-making process? Where would you like God to be? What do you want from God?
- What concerns do you have about the outcome of your decision? Can you share that concern with God?

## Contemplation

While the choices we are confronted with and the decisions we make in young adulthood seem to hold the power to drastically affect the course of our lives, the relationship we have with God need not be derailed by anything that does or does not happen as a result of those decisions. If we get off track, we can always reconnect with the desires, the longings, the call toward God that is at the heart of every important decision we make and, indeed, in everything we do and everything we are.

- How have your feelings toward your self as a young adult changed as a result of the writing you have done?
- Have your feelings toward God changed in the light of this awareness?
- What would you like to embrace or reclaim from your young adult self?
- What might you say to God or ask of God about your young adulthood?

# CHAPTER 14
## Marriage and Significant Relationships

A long-term love commitment has much in common with a commitment to a faith tradition. Both involve dedicated practice, a willingness to lead as well as serve, and an awareness of something greater than the sum of its parts: a spiritual presence. People in loving, committed relationships are drawn in by attraction, sustained by ritual, comforted by familiarity, and yet engaged and challenged by a deepening sense of mystery. Looking for God in the midst of a marriage or significant love relationship would seem to be an easy task, if we start with the assumption that God is love, and we love our partner. However, sometimes the daily circumstances of life cloud over the spiritual foundation that all partnerships rest on. Whether writing about a current relationship or one in the past, a relationship that is painful or pleasurable, use the material in this chapter to explore the significant relationship or relationships in your life, seeking to rediscover a sense of God's presence within them.

If you wish to work more specifically on a certain aspect of your current situation, chapter 30 addresses the issues related to an existing point of tension or ways in which you feel particularly blessed in a relationship. For more details on dealing with difficult relationships, see chapters 21, 22, and 25–28.

### Reflection

Close your eyes for a moment, and visualize you and your partner standing together, then open your eyes, keeping this image in your thoughts. Holding an image of the two of you, reflect on these questions: How are you standing? Are you touching? Are you facing each other or side-by-side? Imagine yourself looking at your partner, making eye contact. Pay attention to your feelings right now, as you look at each other.

- How do you feel toward this person?
- What are your hopes and dreams for your partner?
- What are your hopes and dreams for yourself?
- Do these hopes and dreams you each hold conflict or interact?
- How is God present in these hopes and dreams for you, for your partner?

## Pen in Hand

Write the story of how you met. Describe the setting, the atmosphere, the way you were feeling right before you realized that this person would be important in your life. You may have known this person for a long time before the relationship became "serious." Choose a moment when you gave your heart and moved toward love. Let yourself feel this movement again. Invite God into this flow of love toward another. Write down any details that still hold emotional power for you. What did you say? What did s/he say? Or was the connection you made all in a glance? Go deeply into that moment in your writing.

## Noticing

- How do you feel about reliving this experience of falling in love?
- How hard was it to remember how you felt?
- Are there details that you now remember, that you had forgotten over time?
- How could that initial experience and the feelings that attended it be part of your relationship now?
- Where was God when you met your partner?

## On the Path

Turn your attention to your relationship with God through the lens of this significant love relationship. When God is consciously invited into a partnership, the dynamic shifts from that of a dyad to a triad. Sacred space with room for Mystery, possibility, and transformation opens up. Every relationship, even those that do not consciously and actively welcome God's presence, are nevertheless opportunities to experience

God's grace. As you write, begin to discern where God has participated in your life as someone committed to another, growing in the love of God's embrace.

As you write, remember to keep the focus on yourself, not on your partner. Although your partner is part of the triad, for now you are writing to learn more about who you are as part of this triad, not who someone else is.

Write about what you have learned about yourself spiritually, as you journeyed with another person through life. How has your relationship been a spiritual practice for you? Ask yourself:

- What spiritual lessons have you learned from being in this relationship?
- In what ways has your relationship with God played a part in your role as a partner?
- How would you like God to be present to you as you journey on this path?
- Where would you like to go from here?

## Contemplation

Over the course of a relationship that is paradoxically both intimate and taken for granted, it's easy to forget to look for God's presence in our actions, the presence of our partner, and in the opportunities for grace that arise whenever connections between people occur. As you review the graced history of your marriage/significant relationship, ask God to continue to show you those moments of intimate grace. Remind yourself of the gifts you've received from the relationship, and place them in God's continuing, loving embrace.

- How are you feeling about your experience as a partner in a relationship?
- Are there things you would like to share with your partner, either in person or in prayer, or in writing?
- What would you like to embrace or change about how you participate in your personal relationship as a spiritual practice?
- What might you say to God or ask of God about your part in this personal relationship?

# CHAPTER 15
## The Single Life

Being single, or not in a partnered, committed relationship, brings its own rewards and challenges. It creates an uncluttered space for intimacy with God. There is an independence in being single, the ability to act from authentic desires, free from compromise. The need for solitude, so necessary for time with God, is more easily assuaged in a single life. The single path also requires the courage to venture un-companioned into new territory; it is not simply a path of avoidance or aversion to risk. When being single is embarked upon as a choice to be alone rather than settling for a partnered relationship that does not sustain or bless us, then the blessings are many and the possibilities for discovery, joy, and communion with God, wide open. If you have chosen a single path, either over a lifetime or for certain phases of your life, then an examination of how this choice informs your spiritual journey offers an opportunity for recognition of your well-earned wisdom, maturity, fortitude, and a celebration of the gifts that independence can offer.

### Reflection

Spend some time in reflection on your life of singleness. What qualities does being single bring to your life? What are the gifts you are most aware of? In what ways has the freedom offered by your independence formed your life, in terms of decisions you have made, paths you have chosen, and ways of being that you have explored and embraced? How has being single affected your creativity, your vocation or career, and your relationship with God?

- What are the feelings that arise when you think about your single life?
- What are your hopes and dreams for your life in the future?
- How do you celebrate your singleness?
- Have you shared your experiences of being single with others?
- How is God present in your singleness?

## Pen in Hand

Take fifteen minutes or so, or longer if you need it, to write the story of how you came to be single (a choice that may be made once, or successively over time, as relationship opportunities arise). Examine the aspect of choice: How much did your conscious awareness of making a choice play a part in your being on this path? How have you revisited this choice over the course of your life? Do you remember a specific event or experience that affected your choice? What were the feelings then, and how are they similar or different to the feelings you have now about this path?

## Noticing

- How do you feel about reliving this experience of choosing to be single?
- How much did it feel like a conscious choice?
- How much does it still feel like a choice?
- What is the most important outcome of this choice for you?
- Where was God when you chose the path of being single?

## On the Path

Use this time to write to God about your life of being single. Describe what the rhythm of your days is like in light of your chosen path, and what the larger rhythms and patterns of your life have been. What aspects of your life that you now enjoy or that you feel are gifts are specifically related to the fact of your being single? Your career or vocation? Where you live, how you design your days, the relationships you have formed with friends, family, or community? Your faith? Write as if you have been asked to share what this path of being single is like for someone who is considering it. Offer your experience, your wisdom, and the rewards. Don't exclude the things that have been hard or challenging, or any doubts, grief, or regrets, if any. Your listener (God) is interested in hearing what is in your heart.

Ask yourself:

- What spiritual lessons have you learned from the path of being single?
- In what ways has your relationship with God played a part in your single life?
- How would you like God to be present to you as you continue to journey on this path?
- Where would you like to go from here?

## Contemplation

In many societies the path of being single is the path less traveled. Often there is no easy way to talk about or share what this path is like, except perhaps with others on a similar path. Yet God is always listening, always nonjudgmental, always ready to hear both the good and the hardships, the joy and the doubt, knowing that it's all part of a life deeply lived. God models for us the love that we seek to give and receive from others: unconditional, unfettered, and boundless.

- How are you feeling about your experience of being single?
- Are there aspects of being single that you would like to explore in more depth? How might you do that? (for instance, in spiritual direction, more writing, prayer)
- Do you have a community of people you can share with, or a friend? Are you interested in creating a community?
- How might you nurture yourself spiritually as someone who is single?

# CHAPTER 16
## Parenting

Parenting as a spiritual practice teaches us about what it means to protect, respect, and to care for another. Although parents are concerned with the multitude of details involved in the practical aspects of raising a child (and are busy trying to survive the experience with their health and happiness intact), parents are also involved in the formation of another person's spiritual development, as well as their own. This remains true long after the children have grown into adulthood, because the parenting role is not bound by time, only shaped by it in certain ways according to what each child needs at each stage of their lives. That makes parenting an awesome responsibility as well as a great blessing.

**Reflection**

Think about your role as a parent. Imagine yourself "parenting." What's the first image that comes to mind? Stay with this image for a few moments. What feelings arise? What are you doing? Where are you, and who are you with? Is there another adult in the picture, or are you the only adult in this image? What are you thinking about? Think about whether or not this image is representative of your overall role as a parent.

- What is your reaction to the image that first came to mind? Why?
- How does your role as parent extend beyond time you actually spend with your children? How do you feel about that?

- If you are the only adult in your image, how does that feel? If someone is there parenting with you, how does that feel?
- How is God present in your children's lives?
- How might God be more of a part of your parenting journey?

## Pen in Hand

Write the story of how you came to be a parent. Did you give birth? Adopt? Did you become someone's guardian? What was your journey toward parenthood like? Imagine the moment when you first accepted the responsibility of parenthood in your heart. This may have happened when you found out you were pregnant, or decided to adopt, or first saw or met the child you would be parenting. What was that like? Or perhaps this moment of opening your heart to this relationship, this child, and accepting your commitment came later, long after the physical fact of birth, or of legal or physical responsibility. Describe this moment. If you are a parent of more than one person, feel free to write about each one, or as many as you wish to write about at this time.

## Noticing

- How do you feel about reliving this experience of becoming a parent?
- What do you notice in your body as you think about parenting?
- What would it feel like to share this memory with your child?
- How is that initial experience of parenthood and the feelings that attended it a part of your role as a parent now?
- Where was God when you became a parent?

## On the Path

Now turn your attention to your relationship with God as part of the ongoing spiritual practice of parenting. God can be the source of patience, strength, nourishment, and even humor that all parents need. Finding God in our daily parenting, however, can be more challenging than finding God on a silent retreat. Yet God is in the details of schooling, clothing, and feeding a child, as well as in the large, open, silent spaces of contemplation. Write about what you have learned about yourself spiritually as a parent. How has parenting been a spiritual practice for you? Ask yourself:

- How has parenting impacted your spiritual sense of self?
- How has parenting impacted your relationships with others?
- How has parenting impacted your relationship with God?
- How has parenting affected your feelings about faith community?

## Contemplation

It's easy to forget as a parent caught up in the daily joys and sacrifices of raising children that God is available as a source of strength, wisdom, and comfort—how fortunate parents are to not be God! Instead, parents are conduits of God's love, both giving and receiving grace in the spiritual practicing of raising children. By inviting God to be with us in our parenting, all involved—parents, children, and those around us—are blessed.

- How are you feeling about your experience as a parent?
- Are there things you would like to examine in your role as parent? How might you do that? (for instance, in spiritual direction, more writing, prayer)
- What would you like to embrace or change about your spiritual practice of parenting?
- How might you nurture yourself spiritually as a parent?

# CHAPTER 17
## Education

Ask the question of a random group of people: "Have you ever had a bad time in school?" Sit back while the stories spill out. Yet the same result occurs if you ask, "What have you most enjoyed learning?" The stories abound: I loved learning how to play the piano; I loved learning about marine biology; I loved learning how to read.

Teachers and systems of learning have tremendous power to affect the course of a creative and intellectual life. A harsh critique can wound, while a loving, attentive analysis can spur a student on to more learning, to greater challenges. A learning system that honors all learning styles can facilitate real growth, while a poorly designed system leads to apathy and disengagement. Whatever our particular situation as learners happens to be, its impact on our spiritual development and our relationship with God is worth examining. The ability to think abstractedly, to create, to reason critically, and to hold and examine both the past and the future in our consciousness are uniquely human attributes and a powerful pathway to God. If the experience of learning has been positive, then a valuable avenue of connection is available as part of the whole spiritual journey. If the experience of learning has been negative, then the experiences of creativity, intellectual analysis, and self-expression are impacted detrimentally, and a pathway to God is shut off.

### Reflection

Think about a time when you really enjoyed learning something. This could be anything from an academic subject or discipline, to learning how to throw a baseball, or cook a meal. What is the setting? What are you studying? What is your role? Is it participatory? Are you in a group? How old are you? What are you doing physically? Writing? Listening? Or?

- How did you feel as you learned this new subject?
- Was it difficult to think of something you really enjoyed learning?
- Is this memory more typical or less typical of your educational experience overall? Why is that?
- Where is God in this learning experience?
- How does it feel to remember enjoying learning something new?

## Pen in Hand

Write about a time when learning something left you with a sense of promise or excitement. This might or might not have occurred in a traditional educational setting. Describe what you were learning, how it came about, what your sense of self was as you learned. Describe the teacher, if there was one, but keep the focus on yourself. Describe how you felt during this experience. You may of course also write about a current learning situation, if the feelings of hope, promise, and excitement apply.

## Noticing

- Does what you learned play a part in your current life?
- How has this positive learning experience affected the rest of your life?
- What feelings did you notice as you wrote about this experience?
- Is there anything you are thinking of studying or exploring now?
- Where was God in this learning experience?

## On the Path

When we learn, the experience of learning is as essential to our spiritual development and our connection to God as the results of our learning.

Learning requires that we engage our minds in order to process information, our bodies as we form new connections in our physical understanding and kinetic memory, our consciousness in order to fully absorb the implications of what we are learning, and our creative spirit, because that is how we make new connections between existing facts and forms of knowledge. God calls us into our whole being when we learn. That's why the way we approach and feel about learning is even more important than what we learn. Write about how you feel about learning. Include what you don't want from a learning situation, based on your memories of unhappy or unfruitful experiences. Write, as well, about what you do want from a learning situation, based on positive experiences, or on what you envision an ideal learning experience to be. Then write about what it is you would still like to learn. Describe a concrete skill or knowledge base, as opposed to spiritual or interpersonal lessons about life. Choose something that requires learning with your whole self: thinking, creativity, and "doing." This could include writing, speaking, using your hands, using your body, or all of these. Write about why you want to learn this particular subject, even if you want to "just because" or it seems fun. Learning is a gift that, when grounded in the concrete forms of human culture and imbued with an awareness of the spirit, can open a door into the sacred.

- How have your learning experiences impacted your spiritual sense of self?
- How do you think God feels about you as a learner? About learning?
- What would you still like to learn? How might you go about that?
- What prevents you from learning this subject? What might you say to God about that?

## Contemplation

Although education is usually focused on the pragmatic, people bring both the practical and the spiritual aspects of who they are to everything they do and everything they learn, whether consciously or not. You have now spent some time paying attention to who you are as

a learner, how you feel about learning, and what your desires are for
future learning. Invite God to help you recognize and embrace your
most human qualities that are an essential part of learning: imagination, curiosity, willingness, and dedication, as you choose the learning
experiences that await us every day of our lives.

- How are you feeling about your experiences in learning?
- Are there aspects of your educational history you would like to
  spend more time on?
- How would you go about exploring the possibility of learning
  something new?
- How might you bring your feelings and experiences about
  learning to God?

# CHAPTER 18
## Work History

Work, for most of us, is one of the defining features of adulthood, but people haven't always perceived their work as part of their spiritual path. It can be difficult to locate any sense of the spirit in our daily tasks, our struggles for financial stability, and our career concerns. We may feel this way particularly if we don't have a role in a religious context, or work within one of the professions more commonly accepted as a "helping" profession, such as health care. Spending time offering our skills, talents, and energy in a way that contributes to the common good, as well as providing for our own material needs, is an ideal many of us strive for. How can we recognize God as *part* of what we do rather than as something *outside* of what we do each working day? Exploring the trajectory of our career history can offer us new ways of discovering where God has been as we have made our way in the world of work. (Issues related to a current work situation or calling are discussed in section 6, "Mapping the World of Work.")

### Reflection

Reflect on times over the course of your working life when you felt in total alignment with the kind of work you were engaged in. A time when you felt truly at home with yourself and in your work. If you've never felt in alignment with your work, think back to a time when you were engaged in some kind of task that felt truly engrossing and made you happy, regardless of whether it could be classified as "work" in the traditional sense. This may include some kind of art, a task centered on your home or garden, taking care of animals, or challenging yourself physically. Place yourself in the scene that comes to mind. What are you doing? What do your surroundings look like? When were you doing this work—recently? A long time ago? Are you alone or with other people? What is that like?

- How do you feel as you revisit this time?
- Was it difficult to think of work you really enjoyed doing?
- Is this memory representative of your overall work history?
- Where is God in this work experience?
- How does it feel to remember enjoying your work?

## Pen in Hand

Reflecting on our career history can uncover themes that echo through our working life. We bring values, desires, and expectations to each new task or job situation in hope of finding meaning and even joy. If you have tried many different kinds of work, what similarities do you notice, not necessarily in the type of work, but in how you felt about the work? Are there similar values, desires, or expectations that you hold that pertain to each job? If you have stayed on one career path, what are the values, desires, and expectations that first led you to this path and that are still true for you today? Write about these themes for fifteen minutes, listing what these values, desires, and expectations are and what they mean to you in terms of your work. If you have time or want to continue, describe how they have played a role in your work history.

## Noticing

- What is it like to articulate the values, desires, and expectations you have had for yourself in your work history?
- From where did these values, desires, and expectations originate?
- How hard or how easy has it been to hold on to your values, your desires, your expectations throughout your working life?
- What feelings did you notice as you wrote about these themes?
- What other important themes might be added to this list?

## On the Path

It's natural to want to use our gifts and energies in the spirit of compassion, peace, and joy, regardless of the kind of work we do. Seeking God in the midst of work opens up possibilities for new ways to both discover and use the gifts we have been given. If we start by paying attention to how we feel, where we may have noticed God's presence, we can move from there into a deeper awareness of where and how God may be calling us toward more connection, greater fulfillment. The times when we felt most disconnected and unhappy in our work have not been wasted, for they have a message for us about what it is we need or desire from our work. Times of great joy offer us insights into where we are called to focus our energy and give of ourselves. Recognizing the presence of God in our work history helps us realize that we have not worked in vain or worked alone. Even if work has felt empty at times, or directionless, or frustrating, we have still labored in the light of God's love.

Take a few moments to think about how you got started in your career, vocation, or profession. What motivated you to make this choice, or choices? What were your concerns? What were your hopes? Write about the factors that went into your job decision. Include practical issues such as money, location, your qualifications, and so on. Also include the less tangible issues, such as how you hoped you would feel about your work, what you believed about the importance of the work, and so on. You can repeat this exercise for each job change you have made, if you wish.

- How has your work history impacted your spiritual sense of self?
- Has anything in your work history helped you feel closer
  to God?
- What feelings do you want to share with God, about God's
  presence in your work history?
- How might your relationship with God have played a part in
  your work that was not apparent to you at the time?

## Contemplation

We can waste precious mental and spiritual energy by second-guessing or berating ourselves for work or job choices we have made in the past. Focusing on the lessons we have learned about ourselves and our work is an opportunity to know God and is a more fruitful use of our time and resources. We can also replenish ourselves for the continuing work journey ahead, when we connect with God as an integral part of who we are in the world of work, not as something separate, to be kept for more "spiritual" settings. God is with us in all settings, including the workplace.

- How are you feeling about your work history?
- Are there aspects of your work history you would like to spend more time on?
- How would you go about exploring the possibility of finding new ways of aligning your spiritual identity with your work identity?
- Would you like to bring your feelings about work to God? What would you say?

# CHAPTER 19
## Midlife

Midlife is often a time of re-evaluation. Relationships, career choices, lifestyle, even faith communities and our relationship to God can be subject to review. Questions begin to press in: Am I doing what I want to do for the rest of my life? Are these the companions I wish to travel with? Is it too late to change? When will it be my turn? What is my relationship with God now, and what would I like it to become? For some, this process results in a reaffirmation of the course already set in place; for others, everything gets tossed overboard and a new direction is charted. In either case, where is God in this process?

## Reflection

Whether you are approaching, in the midst of, or reflecting back on midlife, contemplate the images that come to mind when you think about being "middle-aged." How do you see yourself? In what ways are you different from other times in your life? What does middle age mean for you physically? What does it mean in your relationships? How does middle age affect you spiritually? What are your priorities? Where do you put your energy, your attention?

- How do you feel about being in midlife?
- What might be an advantage of midlife?
- What might be a disadvantage?
- Where is God in your middle years?
- What are your hopes and dreams for this time in your life?

## Pen in Hand

Take a few moments to think about what you like about midlife. What blessings does this time bring; what gifts? Write for fifteen minutes about what you believe to be the advantages, the blessings of midlife. What is available to you now that wasn't in earlier years? What freedoms, what choices do you have, now that you are in midlife? What skills have you acquired? What lessons have you learned? What are you grateful for? If writing about the future from a younger perspective, write about what you hope for. If midlife is behind you, write about how you remember those years.

## Noticing

- Is it difficult to focus on the positive aspects of midlife?
- Are there things you would do differently?
- What do you appreciate now that you didn't appreciate when you were younger?
- What feelings did you notice as you wrote about these blessings?
- Would you like to offer these feelings to God? How can you do that?

## On the Path

Choose an aspect of midlife that has helped you connect with God. It might be your role as parent, your sense of fulfillment at work, or a moment of awareness of time passing as you grow older. Describe the setting, the circumstances leading up to this experience, and how you have carried and integrated this experience forward into your life since then. Try to discern what it is about this particular midlife experience that brought you to an awareness of God. How did being who you are at this time in your life create room for this experience? As you write, hold an image of yourself during this experience. If this experience is something that has not been a part of your consciousness recently, write about why this might be the case, and how you feel about that. If you are having difficulty locating such an experience in your midlife, then write about a time when you felt most in alignment with every aspect of your life: your desires, your energy, your gifts, your relationships. You may want to ask yourself:

- How has midlife affected your spirituality?
- What about midlife (based on how you imagined this phase of your life to be) has been different than what you expected? How do you feel about that?
- What feelings do you want to share about this phase of your life?
- How might your relationship with God have played a part in your midlife that you were not aware of at the time?

## Contemplation

Taking the time to contemplate and write about our midlife experiences opens the door to an awareness of God that we might otherwise have missed. Time can feel compressed in midlife, as we peddle furiously away from the freedom and confusion we felt as less-encumbered, less responsible youth, and toward the threshold of older age, freed from the need to establish oneself financially and to launch children into the world. We are so busy with midlife responsibilities: demands on our time from aging parents, children, partners who are also building careers, ever-rising demands from bosses, and so on, not to mention our own growing desire for intimate and creative connection with our spirit. Taking time for ourselves to connect with God can prove vital to our spiritual, emotional, and physical health.

- How are you feeling about midlife?
- What aspects of your midlife experience would you like to honor?
- What aspects of your midlife experience are in need of healing?
- What feelings about midlife would you like to bring to God?

# CHAPTER 20
## Elder-life

Elders tend and feed the steady flames warming the temple of the spirit, even as the temple of the body enters the final transition toward reunion with God. The spiritual fire that warms the elder-life is fed with memory, wisdom, freedom from old roles, and the powerful fuel of love. Elders celebrate the rewards of longevity: deep friendships, release from cultural pressure to achieve, a larger perspective on life. These gifts sustain elders as they encounter the widening spiritual path of grief: loss of parents, partners, and friends to illness; their own diminishing capacities and of those they love; loss of a familiar way of life. The journey into grief carries with it another invitation: a journey into a closer walk with God.

If you are not an elder yet, use this section to consider what you hope for at that stage of life. What attracts you about those years? Where will God be in the elder years of life?

## Reflection

Whether you are approaching or are in the midst of elder-life, contemplate the images that come to mind when you think about being an "elder." How do you see yourself? In what ways are you different from other times in your life? How are you changing physically? Who are you in relationship with? How has your spiritual life changed? What are your priorities? Where do you put your energy, your attention?

- How do you feel about being an elder?
- What might be an advantage of being an elder?

- What might be a disadvantage?
- Where is God in your elder years?
- What do you hope and dream for in this time of life?

## Pen in Hand

Think about what you like about elder-life. What blessings does this time bring; what gifts? What are you grateful for? What is available to you now that wasn't part of your life before? What freedoms or choices do you have, now that you are in elder-life? Write for fifteen minutes about these gifts. Also include what blessings and gifts you now have to offer the world: What skills have you acquired? What lessons have you learned? What wisdom do you carry and embody?

If you are writing about the future from a younger perspective, write what you hope for during this time of life.

## Noticing

- What is it like to focus on the positive aspects of elder-life?
- Are there things you would do differently?
- What do you appreciate now that you didn't appreciate when you were younger?
- What feelings did you notice as you wrote about these blessings?
- Would you like to offer these feelings to God? How can you do that?

## On the Path

Moving toward the final part of the life journey, guides are more important than ever for how to go from here. For elders, guides who are "further along the path" may or may not be available in our present lives. Yet people have forged this path before. The collective wisdom and experience of grandparents, parents, and other people who have served as wise elders in the past now have much to offer us, along with the wisdom and experience of those elders who walk this journey with us side by side as current companions. Our own inner wisdom has been nurtured by these honorable elders, as we become honorable elders in turn. Who has served as a role model for you as you discern what this stage of life might look like, how you want it to proceed, and where God might be found?

Choose someone from your current life or from the past whom you now look to, recognize, and honor as a wise elder. What role does or did this person play in your life? How did the way this person lived as an elder impact your own sense of who you are now and how you wish to shape this final journey? What do you recognize in yourself that you also recognize in this person? If you are having difficulty thinking of someone, then describe what such a person might be like: how they would act toward you, what you might ask of them, what you would want from them. You may want to ask yourself:

- How has this person shaped and informed your elder identity?
- What did this person teach you about aging? About dying?
- How did this person relate to God? What has that meant for you, in your own relationship with God?
- How might you invite the presence, gifts, companionship, and wisdom of this person into your own life?

## Contemplation

Traveling with God in the company of others, the challenges, sorrows, and uncertainties of aging don't disappear. Yet the obstacle that is the fear of the unknown becomes a navigable river instead of a bottomless chasm, as we rely on wise guides, both present and gone before, as well as our own inner and well-earned wisdom. The journey becomes a celebration of all that has been surmounted, of all that has been experienced, of each moment of grace in a life lived in the loving presence of God.

- How are you feeling about elder-life?
- What aspects of your elder-life experience would you like to honor?
- What aspects of your elder-life experience are in need of healing?
- Would you like to bring your feelings about elder-life to God?

# Section 4

## *Recognizing and Navigating the Landscape of Experience*

*Spiritual writing expands the interior conversation of consciousness to include your relationship with the sacred. You are no longer alone on the quest, or on paper. You are in conversation with something you perceive as beyond, or deep within, yourself. It is this inclusion of the sacred that spiritualizes the writing.*

—Christina Baldwin, *Life's Companion: Journal Writing as a Spiritual Quest*

Most of my life I have longed for a house. Not just any house, but a house that only exists in my dreams. The details change over time: it may be built in the trees, perched on a mountainside, or in a suburban neighborhood, or on an urban street. In my imagination, each version of this dream house has something I covet as well as something I find wrong with it, preventing me from acquiring it. Either I can't affort it, or someone else lives in it, or it's unsuitable in some other way. For me this unobtainable house represents many life themes: missing the past; family; a deep desire to belong; a longing to alleviate the sadness that has occurred and continues to occur in my life, as it does in every life.

Significant themes interweave throughout our life journey like a reoccurring motif or a familiar feature on the landscape, offering opportunities to learn important life lessons. Over the course of time, even though they may appear in different guises, we visit and re-visit these experiences, just as my myriad dream houses all contain the same

ongoing quest of finding a home. These themes might include loneliness, grief, how we relate to and feel about our bodies, guilt, or forgiveness. The lessons learned from these themes may be centered in
personal experience or in experiences shared with others. Either way,
God is present in the landscape of our lives, as we navigate the familiar
scenery as well as the unfolding mystery that is the spiritual journey.

The themes in this next section are separated into categories,
although there are no neat boxes or columns on the spiritual journey.
Still it can be helpful and prove fruitful to focus our prayerful attention more closely on these features of our spiritual landscape and
examine the presence of God in each.

Because this section explores experiences of the heart, ask God
for strength, companionship, or simply God's presence as you delve
into these themes more deeply.

# CHAPTER 21
## Disappointment, Loss, and Grief: Shades of Sadness

There are many shades of sadness; they weave through our lives like the wild grasses a bird uses to weave a nest. The loss of a friend who moved away, a job promotion not received, a beloved pet that died, a divorce after many years of marriage, the death or illness of a loved one—these are all events on the spiritual journey that weigh on the heart and cast shadows on the path. Yet whether grief is enfolded in the loss of love, or disappointment in a hoped-for opportunity; whether loss visits as a door shut against us or a choice not granted, the shades of sadness woven into our lives are also filled with God's abiding presence.

The themes of disappointment, loss, and grief begin in childhood and continue to appear, in varying guises, throughout our life. Yet through all of these shadows, we are invited to move closer to God, to know that we do not venture alone, that we are sustained in grace.

### Reflection

What grief, loss, and/or disappointment currently weighs the most on your heart? Chances are this question will readily summon either a memory or a current situation; either way, whether the experience is happening in present time or occurred long ago, honor the reality of your feelings.

Take a few moments to enter into these memories or your current experience. Invite God to be with you in these moments, and ask for what you need or want from God.

- How immediate are these feelings and memories for you? Have they been affected by time, or are they still fresh? Are you experiencing the immediacy of a grief, loss, or disappointment?
- How much are these feelings and memories a part of your current, daily life?
- How does this experience connect with any other experiences?
- What would it be like to share your feelings with someone?
- What would it be like to share your feelings with God?

## Pen in Hand

Choose a situation or experience of grief, disappointment, or loss for you, regardless of when this situation or experience actually took place. Hold this situation or experience in your heart as you begin to write. Describe the details of the situation: tell the story of your grief, loss, or disappointment. Remember, you are writing to a patient, loving, affirming listener. Use concrete images and descriptions: What is the setting? Who are the people involved? How old are you? Use these details to help anchor you in the moment and to maintain some objectivity as you open yourself to these feelings. Write for fifteen minutes. Sometimes it is difficult to choose only one instance to write about. Start with what feels most pressing. You may repeat this exercise again later with a different situation or experience, if you wish.

## Noticing

- Are you surprised at what you chose to write about? Why or why not?
- How has this experience affected your relationship with God?
- How has this experience affected your sense of self?
- Were there any unexpected feelings that you noticed as you wrote about this experience?
- How can you offer these feelings to God?

## On the Path

The pain and sense of aloneness generated by the human reality of loss can lead to a need to surrender to a spiritual reality that transcends our immediate suffering. Offering our anguish to God is the first step in sharing the burden of grief, hurt, or feelings of abandonment and lost hopes. By entering into the immediacy of the feelings and writing about them, we may be able to renew hope, find consolation, and begin to heal. In this next exercise, write about what blessings might result from your experience of grief and loss. We often hear that "when one door closes, another door opens." Describe the door that you would like to see opened. Does it involve a change in a relationship with someone? Does the door open to a new set of circumstances, a new awareness of God? A transformed sense of self and purpose? What do you wish for yourself, as a result of the grief, loss, and disappointment you have experienced? Ask yourself:

- What do you think God might want for you now?
- What do you want for yourself?
- What are the connections between your desires and God's desire for you?
- How might you begin to discern how grace can enter into and transform your pain?

## Contemplation

Reflection, writing, and prayer about our experiences of grief and loss allow us to enter into and then move through our pain, like walking through a shadowed landscape into the light. This process doesn't erase our feelings, but it can ease them, allowing us to honor and learn from them. By envisioning and articulating what we hope for, we are able to place our experiences in the larger continuum of a life held in God's loving hands. These exercises may have opened you to some painful feelings. Spend some time comforting and taking care of yourself, if you need to.

- How are you feeling now? Do you need to spend some time in prayer or in sharing with a trusted friend or spiritual companion?
- Do you want to spend some more time writing?
- How might you take care of yourself right now?
- How might you bring your feelings of grief and loss to God?

# CHAPTER 22
## Trust/Lack of Trust

Trusting is like holding out our hand in peace to the stranger next to us, not knowing if they will grasp our hand with love or slap it away. Will you be the first to hold out your hand? If it is slapped away, will you hold it out again, or turn to someone else? If your hand is held in love, will you continue to offer it to other strangers? How will you decide in the future whom you hold your hand out to? Why hold it out at all? What is gained, what is lost? All of these questions arise each time we trust, yet we continue to hold out our hands, because God calls us to trust, and to trust again. Being with God is not a passive stance; God's hand reaches out, and we reach back, trusting that it will not be slapped away. Practicing trusting is practicing being with God.

The issue of trust pervades our life on multiple levels. We start out trusting, then learn not to trust, then try to regain a sense of trust, not just once in a linear fashion, but over and over again as we circle through each stage of our lives. Can we trust our parents, our friends, our lovers, our coworkers? What about our religious leaders? Can we trust ourselves to know and do the things that are best for us? Can we trust God? The commitment to a faith community, to the spiritual journey itself, to companionship, or to this writing practice are all indications of willingness to trust. Most of us have had positive experiences of trusting, as well as painful experiences of the violation of that trust. Placing our trust in someone or something makes us vulnerable. Sometimes the temptation is strong to not take any risks at all. The decision to not trust at all means not moving closer to God. Another path open to us involves paying attention and learning from the consequences of trusting, both painful as well as joyful, which helps us more clearly discern the spiritual path toward God. We gain wisdom in these lessons of *trustworthiness*; we learn what is worthy of our trust, and what is not. Sorting out what risks are worth taking from the risks that bring only harm, we cultivate the willingness to trust God, to hold out our hand.

## Reflection

What have been your experiences with trust and lack of trust? Chances are this question will readily summon emotions, memories, even current realities. Take a few moments to enter into these memories or your current experience. Invite God to be with you in these moments, and ask God for what you need or want. If your trust concerns are directly related to your relationship with God and affect your feelings about whether or not you can be safe with God or trust that God cares for you, you may want to share these concerns with your spiritual director or a close friend.

- How has the ability to trust affected your spiritual journey?
- What are some of the positive experiences you have had of trusting?
- What is your experience of trusting God?
- What is your experience of trusting yourself?
- What would it be like to share these experiences with someone? With God?

## Pen in Hand

Write about a time when you doubted the wisdom of trusting, yet you went ahead anyway. Choose a time when you thought for sure that your skepticism would be justified, and then it wasn't. Perhaps you invited a dubious stranger into your home, or you agreed to help someone you knew wouldn't help you in return, or you gave someone who had hurt you repeatedly another chance. Write about what you expected from this act of trust, and then what the outcome was. Perhaps someone paid you back money they owed, or they came through on a promise. Choose a time when the outcome of your trust surprised you. Write about what it was like to have your expectations turned upside down. What effect did that have on you?

Write for fifteen minutes.

## Noticing

- Are you surprised at what you chose to write about? Why or why not?
- How did this experience affect your relationship with God?
- How did this experience affect your sense of self?
- Were there any unexpected feelings that you noticed as you wrote about this experience?
- Would you like to offer these feelings to God?

## On the Path

By committing yourself to this writing exercise, you are choosing to trust that the time you invest in reading and reflecting and writing, the willingness to examine and open yourself to reflection, will prove to be worthwhile. You may not know what you are putting your trust in, or why—only that you have chosen to move forward, to give of your time, energy, focus, and willingness to see what happens. Spend some time writing about this act of trust. Write about how this exercise resembles other times in your life when you have made a commitment to trust something, or someone, or God. How have you trusted yourself, your spirit, and your heart, to the mystery of creating, of communicating, of making connection? You may also want to address these questions:

- What is it like for you to trust the writing process?
- What hopes do you bring to the writing process?
- By trusting the writing process, what do you hope from God?
- What implications does the decision to trust this process have for the rest of your life?

## Contemplation

Writing as a spiritual practice is something you can trust. Because this process is your own, it cannot be violated by anyone else's opinions, judgments, or attempts to interfere with it. The spiritual journey asks us to trust ourselves and from there, to trust God, and from there, to trust those people in our lives whom we allow into our hearts and into the sanctuary of our souls. Through writing and discernment and prayer, we can grow in the wisdom needed to make decisions about where to place our trust.

- What other spiritual practices have you learned to trust?
- How does the issue of trust, or lack of trust, play a role in your creative life? In your personal life?
- How might you foster, or begin to rebuild, trust in your own inner wisdom?
- How might you bring your feelings about trust and lack of trust, to God?

# Chapter 23
## Desire: Fulfilled and Unfulfilled

I have always desired a home of my own. I don't require a specific location, or design, or number of rooms to fulfill my desire. I just know that somehow, my need for home is unmet. In fact, I own a house now. Yet no matter how hard I try, I can't make it feel like the home I have always desired, because what I desire—feeling like I'm *home*—is a state of mind, or the spiritual state of being at home in God, not a physical place.

Desires are often masked in the tangibles of daily life, such as desiring a new place to live, a change in how we look, a different job, or a better standard of living. These desires, while of the world, aren't trivial, yet they often represent more than the thing itself. Through examining the material manifestations of our desires, we can look past them for a glimpse of spiritual desires that aren't always obvious. A desire for a new home may represent the desire to find a new way to rest in God. A focus on how much we weigh or what we look like may represent a desire for a fonder, gentler, relationship with our body as a temple of God. Wanting more money may lead to the discovery of a desire for more love, or greater trust in God. By paying attention to what we have long wanted, we can enter into a conversation with God about the true value and meaning of our desires.

### Reflection

What's the first thing that comes to mind when you ask yourself what it is that you most desire? Don't censor your thoughts, or even begin to place them within the limits of "This is what I desire *but. . . .*" Simply hold this desire in your mind and in your heart for a few minutes.

Spend some time with this desire, addressing it by name and allowing it to be at the forefront of your thoughts and feelings.

- What is the first thing that came to mind? Are you surprised that this particular desire came to mind?
- How much do you believe that desires can be fulfilled?
- What values do you place on desires? Are some "better" or more acceptable than others?
- What is your experience of acting on your desires?
- What is your experience of not acting on your desires?

## Pen in Hand

Spend some time writing about the first concrete desire that came to mind. Name the desire in as much detail as possible. Ask yourself: When did it first appear? How prevalent has it been in your thoughts and your feelings over time? How much do you allow yourself to feel this desire, and how much do you try to push it away? Can you say why this is? Have you ever brought this desire to God?

## Noticing

- Did you write about a desire you believe can be fulfilled?
- How has this particular desire affected your relationship with God?
- Does God play any part in whether or not this desire can be fulfilled?
- What is your general feeling about the place of desire in your life?
- What would it be like to offer these feelings to God?

## On the Path

The conversation with God about our desires is ongoing throughout our lives. What we desire changes as we change and grow. An understanding of how God operates in our lives evolves, as does the ability to discern the many unexpected ways desires are met by God. Spend some time writing about your understanding of how God meets your desires. What does God want for you? What do you want from God? You may approach these questions from your lived experience, your theological understanding, or your own feelings, regardless if they seem to make sense. Write everything you carry in your heart about desire. You may want to address these questions:

- How and when have I shared my desire with God?
- How relevant is this desire to my life today? Have I outgrown this desire, or is it still important enough to keep praying about?
- In retrospect, what desire am I glad remained unfulfilled?
- How much does a sense of what I should or shouldn't desire impact or interfere with what I truly want?

## Contemplation

Acknowledging and writing about our desires makes us vulnerable. Yet this process invites us to be honest and to trust the listener, who is God. Denying, belittling, or avoiding the desires of our hearts won't diminish them; these tactics only shield us from total intimacy with God. Honoring your desires by being honest about them may not result in the answers you hope for, but the engagement with God about your hopes and dreams is an essential part of the spiritual conversation and of discovering what God hopes for you.

- What would you like to do now with your desires? (share them, pray about them, write about them, portray them in art, etc.)
- In what other ways might you bring your desires to God?
- What would it be like to spend some time in silent contemplation about how desire has impacted your life and your relationship with God?

# CHAPTER 24
## Physicality

How do you feel about your body? Do you pay it the attention it needs? Do you see it as a gift from God or a burden? Dancing across the room, holding someone's hand on a walk, even reading this book or moving a pen across paper, our bodies get us where we want to go. Spirit, mind, and body are one, a trinity of blessed humanness. Our experience of physicality is a means of connecting with God, as surely as our minds and our spirits. Even the emotions and experiences we think and write about are contained in our muscles and nerves, and our spirit moves in our very breath.

Human beings are an "embodied" aspect of the Holy Spirit, but the way we feel toward our physical selves is very much a result of culture, family mores, church teachings, and our own relationship with our body. Our physical selves are also imbued with sexual energy, the force that compels us to create a connection with life in a physical way. We may express our sexuality through the sensual enjoyment of nature, touch, music, sexual intimacy, or food. We may have rejected sexual impulses or explored them, with varying results ranging from shame to great joy. We may delight in our ability to move, to dance, to play, or feel awkward at every turn, uncomfortable in our own skin. Most of us will have experienced all of these things at varying times in our lives. We can also discern God's loving presence in our physical selves by paying attention to the times when we felt most at home in our own bodies. Delight in our senses, in physical touch, at pushing our physical limits on a long hike—all of these can speak to us of God's presence.

This topic may raise difficult or troubling emotions for some of us. More general themes that may be related to sexuality, including grief, loneliness, lack of trust, anger, and so on, will be explored in more depth in the following chapters. Try to stay with this chapter first, as it focuses on positive aspects of sexuality that you may find helpful and healing.

## Reflection

What has been your experience of your body over the course of your life? Think about the first time you remember enjoying your body. What were you doing? Where were you? How old were you? What was it about this occasion that made it possible for you to enjoy yourself? If you were with another person, how did that affect the experience? What did your body feel like? What made this experience different from other physical experiences?

- How do you feel about remembering this time?
- How common or uncommon are these experiences and feelings for you?
- How has this experience continued in your life?
- Where was God in this experience?
- What is it like to think about your physical self?

## Pen in Hand

Take a few moments to think about what you liked about your physical self when you were a child. What pleasures were you able to enjoy because of your body? Then move forward to later years, stopping at those times that interest you, and list them. Focus on those times when your relationship to your body has proved fruitful. This might include being physically intimate with another person, enjoying a craft, some pleasure of the senses, or simply being able to walk from here to there. Think about what gifts or blessings you have received or enjoyed as a result of your *physical* presence on this earth, in relationship with God.

## Noticing

- How difficult is it to focus on the positive aspects of your physical self?
- What do you most enjoy about your physical self?
- How has your physicality changed over time?
- What feelings did you notice as you wrote about enjoying your physical self?
- Would you like to offer these feelings to God?

## On the Path

Bodies may be a biological construct, but they are also infused with a generative energy called sexuality that offers a means of connection with God. The word "sexuality" or "sexual" has been distorted, exploited, widely interpreted, co-opted and misused for all sorts of purposes, by all sorts of institutions, throughout the ages. Yet simply put, sexuality is the life energy that courses through our bodies, beckoning us toward creation, procreation, connection with others and with all physical matter, and toward God. Write about your own understanding of what it means to experience sexual energy. Moving from the overall experience of the physical self to the more specific experience of sexual energy, ask yourself: What does your definition of sexuality include? What would you like it to include? Using this definition, write about how you most like to express your own sexuality. Using your own definition allows you to move beyond the limited imagination and strictures of the media, the church, or what our parents told us. We all have a sexual identity just as we all have a spiritual identity, with some things that are common to most of us, and certain things that are as unique as we are in God's sight. Allow yourself to imagine what sexuality would, or could, or does, look like for you. Does it include the way you move? The way you communicate with others? The way you enter into the experience of the senses? Also consider writing about:

- Where and in what ways do you feel free to express your sexuality?

- When might you have felt close to God through the enjoyment of your sexual self?
- What would you like to explore or invite into your sexual life?
- How does your relationship with God play a part in your sexuality?

## Contemplation

Unless we make a practice of it, we can easily forget that we are gifted with physical life, and with that gift are invited to know God in unique ways. Our bodies can be something we ignore or even hide from, as we pursue other methods of spiritual awakening and connection. Yet our bodies, infused with sexual energy, can teach us about what it means to be human; they can offer us ways to reach others and through that experience, reach God, and can remind us of the pleasures of God's world.

- How are you feeling about your body and sexuality?
- What aspects of your physical self and your sexuality might you pay more attention to?
- What aspects of your physical self and sexuality are in need of healing?
- Would you like to bring your feelings about your body and your sexuality to God?

# CHAPTER 25
## Loneliness

Many of us know the paradox of feeling "lonely in a crowd." Similarly, many of us have felt lonely when we least expected it: in a personal relationship, or surrounded by friends, in communal worship, or even during prayer. What's going on? We find ourselves cut off from others, from God, from our ability to companion our own selves. We have wandered off alone. We have looked for companionship and not found it where we had hoped or expected it. In our despair, we lose sight of other paths, other possibilities for connection. Loneliness can only be assuaged when we open our hearts to new ways to rejoin, through the spirit, to life. Whether loneliness arises out of a real experience of abandonment by others, or a deep sense of abandonment by God during a time of suffering, the way back to connection and a sense of companionship may be as close as the person sitting next to us, or as simple as a prayer. When loneliness is a path we have chosen temporarily, as we pursue a call or a vision that leads us away from the company we once held, the relationships we once forged, or even away from an existing personal identity toward a new sense of self, then inviting God to companion us as we venture down the uncharted road means we need not journey alone.

### Reflection

How fresh and immediate is the feeling of loneliness for you? If it is something you are grappling with currently, take a few moments to reflect on the circumstances that brought you to this place. Then, if you're willing, enter into the feeling in a prayerful way, asking God for courage and support. If current loneliness is not an immediate concern for you, reflect on an experience of loneliness in the past, or perhaps the fear of loneliness in the future. Ask yourself if you carry a feeling of loneliness from the past that needs healing and enter into that still-real feeling (again, asking God for courage and support). If nothing from the past feels pressing, you might instead choose to reflect any dread you may feel of looming loneliness, because you are anticipating the loss of someone who has been a companion, or an upcoming change in circumstance that may alter your family or personal relationships.

- How often do you spend time being aware of being lonely?
- How do you mainly experience loneliness? Spiritually? Culturally? In relationships? Physically? In your career/vocation? How else?
- What might be some ways that you hope your loneliness might be eased?
- How does this feeling of loneliness affect your ability to go forward in life?
- What is the connection between God and your loneliness?

## Pen in Hand

Based on your reflections, spend fifteen minutes writing about the characteristics of loneliness as you have experienced them. Place your feeling of loneliness within the context of your imagination. How would you describe the quality of loneliness? What are the colors, the textures, the sounds of loneliness? What does loneliness look like as an image or an object? Is there a place that represents loneliness for you? What is that place like? Is there a kind of weather, a quality of light, or a time of day that personifies loneliness? Write as complete a portrait of your experience of loneliness as you can.

## Noticing

- How do you feel about your portrait of loneliness?
- Are the images and descriptions you chose from recent experience, further in the past, or from the present?

- How does your description resemble your image of God?
- How do you feel after "imagining" your loneliness?
- What would it be like to offer these feelings to God?

## On the Path

Write about how you feel about having been lonely, how you feel that way now, or your concerns about loneliness in the future. Say everything that comes to mind about how loneliness has impacted or will impact your life. Spend some time describing not only the feeling of loneliness, but the effects of loneliness on your personal life, your practical decisions about things like career, vocation, creativity, finding community, and making a home, and your relationship with God. From there, write about what you would prefer instead of loneliness. The point is not to spend time in wishful thinking (if I had that job or that relationship, I wouldn't be lonely), but to ask God for what you would like to receive in order to bear with and hold your loneliness as a part of human experience: things like patience, or the ability to see new opportunities for connection, or courage. Some aspects of the effects of loneliness you might want to consider:

- How has loneliness or the fear of loneliness prevented you from making certain decisions?
- How has the experience of loneliness impacted your spiritual journey?
- How does your experience of loneliness color your feelings about yourself?
- How does your experience of loneliness color your feelings about God?

## Contemplation

Acknowledging and writing about loneliness may stir up other powerful feelings such as anger, bitterness, or envy. If it does, bring those feelings to God as well, for they are all part of the human experience of suffering. Loneliness can feel like a very passive condition that is beyond our ability to change. Yet by choosing to engage in our own experience of loneliness by writing about it, praying, sharing with someone else, or by reframing loneliness through a creative exercise, we befriend ourselves because we take ourselves seriously and show interest in our own well-being. By being willing to investigate our feelings through prayerful writing, we also offer God a way to be our holy companion.

- In what other medium would you like to portray loneliness? (i.e., sculpture, dance, music, poetry, drawing, icon-making, etc.) What would that be like?
- How might your experience of loneliness benefit others?
- How might your experience of loneliness connect you to God?
- Where would you like to go from here?

# CHAPTER 26
## Anger

Like a knotted muscle or a clenched jaw, anger is a powerful indicator that something is out of alignment within our spirit. Recognizing that we are angry at all is often a first step toward processing our anger, yet one many people avoid. Feeling depressed, apathetic, or cynical can feel safer than admitting to and feeling the actual energy of anger. Sometimes we just accept a situation, skipping over the step of acknowledging anger, and ignore what might be an indicator of a need for change. But unexpressed anger harms us and those around us in so many ways. It gets stored in our bodies as tension, stress, and even illness, or we redistribute the toxic effects of anger into our relationships with others, even those unrelated to the anger.

Because anger is uncomfortable, it's easier to ignore it than engage it, but anger can be a helpful companion. In some cases it becomes an energizing force that results in constructive change on our own behalf or for those around us. If our anger is a consequence of our being helpless to change or control a situation, then we can still offer our anger to God: an action that allows us to move from feeling alone in our anger and helpless in the world, to an interactive alliance with God.

Anger can be particularly troublesome when we attempt to wrestle with its appropriateness within the context of many spiritual traditions. Our faith tradition may or may not help us understand the place of anger on the spiritual path. Yet masking, denying, or rationalizing anger robs us of the opportunity to bring to God this most human aspect of who we are.

## Reflection

Think about a time when you were angry. Or focus on something that is making you angry now. Focus on a time related to a specific incident, rather than more generalized anger with "the way things are." Think about what you did, or did not do, as a result of these angry feelings. Were you moved to action? What were the results for you emotionally, spiritually? How did your anger impact your relationship with others? With God?

- What are you aware of in your body as you think about this situation?
- Was it difficult or easy to think of an instance of being angry? Why?
- How much power does this anger still hold for you?
- How do you feel about being angry?
- What does it feel like to consider bringing your anger to God?

## Pen in Hand

Choose a situation that makes you angry today. Rather than getting into a litany of blame ("she said, I said, she said, I said"), focus for fifteen minutes on writing about how your anger might be turned into a benefit, not how you would resolve the actual situation. Turn your anger into a gift. What is positive about your anger? Reframe your anger as something that God has given you as an essential part of being human. Could your anger help you take action in other parts of your life? Could it move you to make changes? Could it help you set personal boundaries? Anger can be transforming, if we ask God to show us how. This doesn't assume that anger should be diluted or made "acceptable." This exercise, however, is about examining the positive use of anger in a God-centered life.

Before you begin writing, ask God to help you understand the gift and role of anger in your spirit, in your human identity. Focus on imagining anger as the first step toward healing: a positive source of energy that can move you from darkness to light. Start your first sentence with: "My anger is a gift from God that I can use to. . . ."

Every time you get stuck or run out of things to say, start a new sentence with the same words, "My anger is a gift from God that I can use to . . . ." If your anger is directed toward God, you may still find this exercise useful. Change the sentence to: "I am angry with you, God. I can use the gift of this anger to . . . ."

## Noticing

- How does writing about your anger as a gift feel to you?
- What answers most surprised you?
- Was it difficult to get started writing? To keep going? Why?
- Has your anger shifted? How?
- How does it feel to share your anger with God?

## On the Path

Anger grounded in the authentic recognition of violation against mind, body, or spirit becomes a means of connecting with God through our sense of injustice. Anger becomes the impetus for reaching for God, who serves as our ally. Reflect now on anger within you that rises from that sense of injustice, whether the focus of that anger is an institution, a governmental system, your faith tradition, or some other group of beliefs.

While this kind of anger can feel global, overwhelming, and irresolvable, there are ways to live with and even move forward using the gifts that anger gives us: new energy for service and social justice work, courage to act authentically, and the powerful reminder that we are all connected as one, both within the context of these larger institutions and in God.

Choose a system that makes you angry enough that your life is affected by your anger. (Remember that this is not necessarily a good or bad thing—it just is.) Write about your relationship with this institution. Begin with some specific details: What is your place within it? How did you come to play a part in it? For how long has this system impacted your life? How long will it continue to impact your life? Then ask yourself these specific questions, and answer them as best you can:

- What kind of spiritual freedom do I feel I have in this system? How is that related to my anger?
- What kind of spiritual freedom do others have? How is that related to my anger?
- Where do I feel God is operating within this system? How is that related to my anger?
- How might I begin, in partnership with God, to work for justice within this system?

## Contemplation

Anger can consume us, or it can transform us. That's true, too, for the systems in which we operate, including families, workplaces, cultures, and faith traditions. Learning to seek God's guidance, support, and patience as we confront our own anger and reckon with the consequences allows us to embrace the gifts of compassion, a sense of mercy and justice, and the sense of ourselves as a beloved member of the human family.

- Misdirected anger can be harmful to all concerned. Spend some time reflecting on how you might find ways to talk about and share your anger with someone you trust.
- How might you stay in alignment with God as you work through your anger?
- How might you express your anger creatively, instead of destructively?
- How might you balance situations that make you angry with those that bring you joy?

# Chapter 27

# Guilt and Shame

When we carry guilt, it's as if we are moving through life clothed in barbed wire. Guilt serves as a barrier against closeness, against forgiveness, against love. When we feel guilty we cannot open our hearts to the spirit. We cannot receive the love we so deserve. We can't even recognize that we deserve it in the first place.

There are two major kinds of guilt. Real guilt is that which is well-earned by our own actions or failure to act. Real guilt is a useful reminder that we can be more than we are; that we are called to be more. Have we purposely hurt someone? Have we knowingly gone against our own moral values? Owning our guilt in these situations and making amends helps us unwrap the barbed wire and return to fullness of life. False guilt is that which has been superimposed on us from outside, whether by an institution, someone else's inaccurate judgment, or by society. Are we in fact feeling guilty for we who are in our very essence? Has someone or something conspired to impose a sense of guilt on us for being who God made us to be?

Discerning the difference between false and real guilt is a first step in healing. For we all carry some of both: false guilt, because we have been judged falsely; and real guilt, because we are human and have made mistakes that have hurt others, ourselves, and our relationship with God. False guilt can be cast aside, if we are willing to no longer accept blame that doesn't belong to us, thus redeeming our true selves. The good news is that real guilt is also redeemable in God: first by our willingness to see clearly, accept what part we have played, ask forgiveness, acknowledge the need for change, and then to act accordingly. Taking the time to investigate the source of our guilt requires courage and a willingness to look dispassionately at the facts, along with a gentle attitude toward our own humanness. From there we can begin to unwrap the barbed wire and live freely again.

## Reflection: False Guilt

False guilt usually carries with it a concomitant feeling of secrecy, which leads to shame, which is an irrational yet powerful cloud that descends on the spirit like black coal dust. False guilt is often discernable by the depth of shame we feel; we are driven to secrecy and shame, because we have been judged for something we can't ever hope to rectify—who we are. We have been judged by others and found wanting, but it is the judgment that is wrong, not who we are. Yet the resulting shame is intense, because we are trapped in a no-win situation. Even if we were to accept blame for whatever we have been accused of, we cannot actually *change* what we have been accused of (because it is a false accusation to begin with), so who we are is driven underground and kept secret from others, ourselves, and from God. Shame occurs in the interior world of heart, body, and spirit; it can only be healed by love. Take a few moments to think about something you feel ashamed of. What have you actually done to bring about this feeling of shame? What is the judgment being made about you? Are you being judged, either by yourself or by someone else, for something you did, or for something you *are*? Opening the door on shame allows us to begin to brush away the dust that overlays our most precious self.

- What about yourself do you keep hidden from others?
- How would you feel about addressing your sense of shame in writing?
- How would you feel about sharing any feelings of shame that you write about with someone else?
- How much do you feel responsible for your feelings of guilt or shame?
- What would it be like to bring these feelings to God?

## Pen in Hand: False Guilt

*You may choose to do this exercise more than once. If so, give yourself time between for reflection, sharing (if available), and prayer.*

Based on your reflections, spend fifteen minutes or so writing about something you feel shame about. This probably won't reside in a specific incident. For instance, you may feel guilty about skipping an important meeting, but you may feel shame for not being thought of as a better employee in general. (You can control whether you skip meetings, but not how others view you as an employee.) Your shame might be located in your overall sense of worth, your sexuality, your gender, your role or place in society, or in your church. Writing about shame is often much more difficult than writing about guilt. Give yourself a few moments or several if needed to center yourself in knowing that God is listening without judgment, with unconditional love. Write for as long as you feel comfortable about the role shame has played in your life.

## Noticing

- How was it to write about this issue?
- What did you learn about yourself?
- What was it like to begin to discern the difference between real guilt and shame?
- How useful is this distinction for you?
- What would it be like to invite God into this process with you?

## On the Path: False Guilt

In the first exercise on false guilt, you spent some time writing about a more comprehensive sense of shame in your life. In this exercise, take some time to imagine yourself being in alignment with your sense of self, in your relations to others, to the world, and to God. Imagine how you would like to proceed from this moment onward, at peace with whatever has caused you to feel falsely guilty, and free from whatever has caused you to feel shame. Write a portrait of who you would be in this new sense of freedom, how your life might proceed when the burden of guilt and shame has lifted. Write about what your relationship with God might be like in this new freedom.

In the second part of this exercise, write about what you believe it would take for you to get from here to there, from the barbed wire to the open meadow beyond. What would you need from yourself? What do you need from God to help you receive this gift of openness and freedom? You might want to write about your thoughts on:

- Who in your life colludes in your sense of shame?
- What action could you take to change that?
- What do you need to help heal your sense of shame?
- What would it be like to speak to God directly about these feelings?

## Reflection: Real Guilt

Real guilt operates on a more practical, reasonable level. Let's say I feel guilty for something I have done: I have broken a promise, broken a law, or violated my moral code. I have determined that I am responsible for this feeling and have accepted dealing with the consequences. Real guilt is something I can grapple with: amends can be made, forgiveness sought, changes can occur to insure no further repetition. Guilt exists in the external world of action, deed, and thought. Think about something you feel guilty about. What part of this guilt is yours? Do you know what actions you might take to absolve you of this guilt? Opening the door on guilt avails us of the opportunity to make amends.

- How would you begin to discern the difference between feeling guilt and feeling shame?
- What do you think about the concept that guilt is usually warranted, but shame is not?
- What aspects of feeling guilty would you like to address in writing?
- What would it be like to share your sense of guilt with someone else?
- Have you considered bringing these feelings to God?

## Pen in Hand: Real Guilt

*You may choose to do this exercise more than once. If so, give yourself time between for reflection, sharing (if available), and prayer.*

Based on your reflections, spend fifteen minutes or so writing about something you feel guilty about. Describe it as matter-of-factly as you can, without trying to defend yourself. Try to pick something more particular ("I didn't visit my mom last week") as opposed to something more global ("I haven't spent enough time with my mom over the last few years"). What were the contributing factors that led to this situation? What were the circumstances? Give details. What were you doing? What was going on around you? What exactly happened as a result of your action or inaction (include what actually happened, not just how you felt).

## Noticing

- How was it to write so "factually" about an instance you feel guilty about?
- How long have you harbored guilt about this incident?
- What did you notice in yourself as you wrote?
- How are you feeling now?
- Would you like to offer these feelings to God?

## On the Path: Real Guilt

In the first exercise on guilt, you spent some time writing about the circumstances related to a particular instance you feel guilty about. In this exercise, take some time to imagine what it would take to make amends for whatever you did, or failed to do, that resulted in feeling guilty. Write a description of the steps that could be taken to alleviate the situation. Stay within the practical, keeping in mind that alleviating our guilt carries with it the responsibility of trying our best not to further hurt others in the process. You may want to include these questions:

- What benefits, if any, are you receiving by not dealing with your guilt?

- What is detrimental about your guilt?
- What do you need to do to make amends?
- How has your relationship with God been affected by your guilt, and how might that change if you make amends?

## Contemplation

Exploring and writing about the powerful topics of guilt and shame can be both freeing and disturbing. While celebrating and embracing any feelings of hope and possibility that you may notice as a result of this spiritual work, also pay close attention to any feelings of inadequacy, sorrow, vulnerability, or other sensitive and painful feelings that may have been evoked by addressing these issues. Give yourself credit for the courage and honesty it takes to tackle these aspects of who we are and how we have lived. You are moving into an ever more open and free relationship with yourself, the world, and God.

- Bring any feelings of darkness, despair, anger, or grief that may have arisen to someone who can support you as you grow (a spiritual director, a trusted friend, a safe group).
- How can you nurture yourself as you work though these issues?
- How might your experience of guilt or shame connect you to God?
- Where would you like to go from here?

# CHAPTER 28
## Forgiveness

Forgiveness stands at the open door of love, beckoning us into her sanctuary with a smile. Whereas guilt and shame drive everything *away* from us as we seek to avoid recognizing our feelings and the connection with others who might "discover" our secrets, forgiveness invites everything *toward* us as we open ourselves to the joys of relief, honesty, and letting down the barriers around our sense of self. Entering into forgiveness transforms us. The act of forgiving doesn't necessarily alter the circumstances that occurred, the blame assigned, or the consequences of actions taken or not taken, but who we are in relation to these things changes. Forgiving others or ourselves isn't easy, however. It requires us to undergo a process of letting go of what we hold too tightly and allowing ourselves to be enfolded in new peace.

How do we get there from here? How can we move from resentment to peace, from pain to hope, and from fear to trust? We can start by examining our own part in the spiraling conditions that brought us to this place of needing and wanting to forgive and by communicating with God about that. We forgive in conjunction with God, not apart from God, and so we can only do our part, while God does the rest. Our part can include prayer, examination of our conscience, and healing our own wounds. Writing about the need and desire to forgive can also help us move closer to that state of grace.

### Reflection

Take a few moments to think about someone you haven't forgiven for something they have done, or failed to do. As you begin to contemplate that person, ask God to be present with you as you hold the image of the two of you. Do not consider yourself alone with this person as you contemplate your need to forgive. God is with you as well, present both in your pain, your resentment, the part of you that is willing to forgive, and the part of you that is unwilling. By your invitation, God is also with the person you wish to forgive.

- If you were surprised by who came to mind when you thought about forgiveness, why do you suppose that is? If it was someone you have long needed to forgive, what does it feel like to have carried this feeling for so long?
- What are your feelings as you contemplate this person?
- How does it feel to bring this person not only into your awareness, but also into God's presence?
- How might your life go forward if you forgave this person?
- What might you ask of God in this situation?

## Pen in Hand

Write a narrative of how your life has been affected by not forgiving the person you've been contemplating. If you want to, write a brief sketch about the circumstances that resulted in your being hurt. If you're not ready to write about this yet, just hold the situation gently in your mind, and move on to writing about this when you're ready. How has the course of your life been altered by this person's actions? How has your life been altered by your lack of forgiveness? How would your life change now if you forgave this person? There is no judgment attached to whether or not you feel "ready" to forgive this person. Just examine the consequences of not forgiving without judging yourself.

## Noticing

- How does the thought of forgiving this person make you feel?
- Does forgiveness feel obtainable, or out of reach? Why?
- How might God be a part of your struggles with forgiveness?
- Do you feel any differently after "imagining" yourself or God forgiving this person?
- What is it like to include God in this process?

## On the Path

Other examples of needing to forgive may not come so readily to mind, but they carry great sorrowful weight nevertheless. We may have not allowed ourselves to consider our need to forgive in situations that are still too painful for us to contemplate; we may want to pray for the possibility of a willingness to forgive, and leave it to God from there. One of the people we most often overlook when we think about who we need or want to forgive is ourselves. In this next exercise, use the same contemplative approach you used in the previous exercise, only imagine yourself as the person you need to forgive. Again, invite God to be with you as you hold an image of yourself, reflecting on whatever it is you have not forgiven yourself for doing, or for failing to do. Then spend half an hour writing to yourself. What is it you haven't forgiven yourself for? Also write to yourself in answer to these questions:

- What might be preventing my ability to forgive myself?
- How has my need to forgive myself affected the course of my life?
- How has my inability to forgive myself affected me spiritually?
- Am I being less, or more, forgiving of myself than I believe God would be? Why?
- How might my life, my relationships with others, and my relationship with God change if I could forgive myself?

## Contemplation

Forgiveness is sacred territory. We embody qualities of the divine when we forgive and when we are forgiven. The willingness to consider the place of forgiveness in our lives takes courage, honesty, flexibility and resilience, and God's loving presence and support. Writing and sharing about our struggles with forgiveness allows us to move into greater freedom from resentment and fear and into grace.

- What aspects of your faith tradition might you draw on as part of learning to forgive?
- How might your forgiveness benefit others?
- How might your experience of forgiveness connect you to God?
- How would it feel to rest in forgiveness?

## Section 5
# *Companions on the Path*

*All of the work of discernment led me to this place. I had thought I was discerning a vocation to priesthood, but in fact I had been discerning my relations to my brother's death, to my husband, to the world I live in, and finally, to myself. I had found the sacred, again, but in different places.*
  —Nora Gallagher, *Practicing Resurrection: A Memoir of Work Doubt, Discernment, and Moments of Grace*

Along with who we are and how we relate to and envision God, our relationships with other people are a defining factor in the shape and feel of our lives. Regardless of how we might long for times of solitude and freedom from the responsibility of interaction, commitment, and care, we can't live without others. Without others, we can't fully realize ourselves as people of God, because God is present in the connections we make, embodied in our human ways of interacting and loving. Relationships are our lot, whether fraught with tension, imbued with joy, weighed down with duty, or filled with creative energy, or all of these things at once. We need to be in relationship if we wish to move beyond the limits of our own capabilities into greater compassion and love.

In this next section we'll explore the circles of relationships that make up our world, from the intimacy of love, to the tussle and pitch that is family, to the wider embrace of human community.

# CHAPTER 29
## Family: Parents, Children, Siblings

Family life can be summed up in a simple grammatical exercise. Read these two prayer-sentences and see which one resonates with you: "Thank God, I have a family to spend time with during the holidays." Or, "Oh my God, I have to spend time with my family during the holidays." Family life is, for most of us, a mixture of both of these heartfelt prayers: blessing and obligation. Both are gifts in their own way, as we grow toward God through the spiritual practice of being in human relationships. At its best, family life involves love, struggle, conflict, forgiveness, empowerment, growth, and so much more. At its worst, families exhibit abusive behaviors and hurt one another in powerful ways.

Placing God at the center of these relationships, as we struggle to find our way in our all-too-human families, can help us find perspective and make choices about who we want to be and how we wish to participate in these relationships. We can find and express heart-centered compassion for our parents, children, and siblings, and for ourselves.

### Reflection

Spend some time thinking about the various roles you hold, or have held, over the course of your life as a member of a family. Choose one role that you would particularly like to explore in prayerful writing. The relationship that you want to explore in this exercise may be in the past now, because of death or separation, which is fine; these relationships, though not active in our present everyday lives, can still hold great significance for us and can live on in our hearts. This may be a relationship based in conflict, or a relationship that feels very joyful right now. Imagine the person you relate to most when in your role, being with you in a familiar circumstance. Imagine yourself relating to this person in the role you play with them: as their child, their parent, or their sibling. What setting are you in? What are you doing? What are you feeling? How do you feel physically? How are you interacting together? Are you talking? What is the atmosphere like?

Now take a few moments to pay attention to your body here and now, as you imagine this scene. Pay attention to your breathing and any other physical sensations you're experiencing.

Holding this image of the two of you in your mind's eye, invite God to be present. If the scene you are imagining is tense, ask God for support, courage, or whatever else you need. If the scene you are imagining is joyful and relaxed, ask God to widen your heart's embrace, to fully take in the gift of this moment.

Now say goodbye to this person, for now. Notice how you feel about leaving their presence.

- Why did you choose this particular person to spend time with?
- How did it feel to be with this person in your imagination?
- What would it be like to explore this relationship further?
- What feelings did you notice, regarding your role as this person's child/parent/sibling?
- Did the quality of the atmosphere change when you asked God to be present?

## Pen in Hand

Take some time to think about the areas in your family life that are the most problematic. (We will focus on blessings in the next exercise.) What situation or family dynamic is the most troublesome to you right now? What concerns you in your role as parent/child/sibling, and in your relationship with this person? This may or may not be a current situation. Sometimes we are most concerned with a relationship that no longer exists, or exists in a different form—such as our relationship with a parent during our childhood, or a relationship with a grown child. Focus on your concern for a few minutes, then spend fifteen minutes writing an account of what it is that troubles you about that relationship. We may have relationships with family members that seem inseparable from our role with them: for instance, we can't see our parent as a fellow-adult instead of as their child. Explain how your role with this person impacts the relationship you might otherwise have with them, and how you feel about that. Then write about how you would go about opening up the dynamic between the two of you into a relationship that includes God. What might change in your relationship and in your identity as a family member as a result?

## Noticing

- How do you feel about your role as parent/child/sibling in relation to this person?
- How does your role impact how you feel about yourself?
- What emotions are present for you in this relationship?
- Do you see your role as parent/child/sibling as inseparable from how you relate to this person? How does that feel?
- How can you invite God into this relationship?

## On the Path

Now turn from focusing on a given relationship to the blessings we have received from our family lives. Even difficult family circumstances bring with them some blessing, no matter how small. In the best circumstances the blessings are abundant. We learn about ourselves, we are given opportunities for service, for love, for patience. Perhaps our gifts were acknowledged and cultivated, or we learned the art of cooperation. Spend thirty minutes writing about the gifts you have received from your family. You may focus on one role or relationship in particular in your writing, or more generally, as a person with many family roles. You may wish to ask yourself:

- What blessing has been the most important to me? Why?
- How have the blessings I have received benefited others?
- How have these blessings affected me spiritually?
- Am I holding on to regret or resentment? How might that affect my ability to recognize blessings?

- How might my relationships with my family and with God change if I could focus on the blessings of family?

## Contemplation

Our roles as parent, child, or sibling impact us on many levels, from the physical to the spiritual. We may have chosen as adults to relate to our families in a radically new way, in the same way we have always done, or we may have chosen not to relate to them at all. Yet whether we see the various members of our family every day or not at all, our relationship with family continues on, in our hearts, our spirit, even our bodies. Bringing to God *who we are* or have been in those roles and who we would like to be helps us to practice with God an emotional and spiritual connection that we can then extend to other people.

- How might you envision a sense of freedom in your family roles?
- What struck you most as you wrote about blessings?
- How do you feel about making room for choices that can affirm you in your family life?
- How might you invite God into your choice-making?

# CHAPTER 30
## Intimacy

"Blessed be the ties that bind." While the concept of binding as blessing may seem like a contradiction in terms, when two people bind their lives together, they become free to move beyond the confines of one heart, one life, into an expansive love that extends beyond the self. Commitment, because it provides safety and the strength and courage of two instead of one, offers a foundation from which to soar.

At some point in our adult lives, we may have chosen to enter into a significant relationship, either in a traditional marriage arrangement, bound by the rule of law as well as sacred vows, or as two people who bind to each other in a partnered, life-long covenant based on a mutual understanding of loving commitment. The bond that results when two people form a relationship differs from all other relationships in their lives, with responsibilities, gifts, and challenges that offer opportunities for developing and nurturing intimacy of the mind, body, and spirit. Who are we in relationship to this commitment? How are we with God in the midst of this covenant with another human being? This chapter assumes that you choose to be in the relationship under discussion and are generally happy. If your relationship is clouded by unhappiness, use the material in this chapter to clarify your feelings and situation. These exercises may also be helpful in pondering a relationship that has ended, or one that you are considering.

### Reflection

Think for a moment about who you were before you entered into your commitment with another person. What was your life like? What were you focused on? Where were you in your faith journey? Now imagine yourself with your chosen partner. Center on a moment, a situation, or experience that conveys the best of your relationship and epitomizes the reason you now choose to be with this person. Feel all of the intensity of your emotions. If you can't think of a reason at this point in time that carries any authentic gladness, then imagine a moment in your relationship when this was that case, and focus on that. Be with this person in your imagination. Then offer this moment with your partner up to God in prayer.

- How does it feel to think about your partner?
- How does it feel to place yourself in the moment you chose?
- How does it feel to bring your partner not only into your awareness, but also into God's presence?
- What would you like to say to this person right now?
- How often are you able to enter into this awareness of love?

## Pen in Hand

Take a few moments to reflect on your relationship as it affects and pertains to your spiritual life. Do you consider your relationship with your partner and your relationship with God as separate from each other, or are they part of a whole? Are there aspects of your relationship that enhance, nourish, model, or otherwise impact your relationship with God or your desire for such a relationship? Conversely, are there ways in which your personal relationship distracts or impedes your spiritual journey or your relationship with God? Explore ways to integrate your personal and spiritual relationships, finding the holy in your partnership and the personal in your communion with God. Write for fifteen minutes about how you see your partnership in relation to your spiritual life, what you find most fruitful, and where you might like to ask God for deeper integration and intimacy.

## Noticing

- How important is it for you, as you write about this, to integrate your personal and spiritual life? Why?

- What do you want to ask of your partner in terms of your spiritual journey?
- What do you want to ask of God in terms of your personal relationship?
- What are your feelings as you reflect on this aspect of your life?

## On the Path

Write about what it means for you to be in a partnership. While remembering the blessings the role of partner brings to you, step outside of the immediate reality and intimacy of your life together and consider all the other aspects of your life that are impacted by the fact that you are in a committed relationship. Ask yourself: How does my being in a committed relationship affect:

- My career?
- My spiritual life?
- My creative life?
- My other relationships?
- My plans for the future?
- Where I live?
- How I spend my time and my money?
- My participation in a faith community?

Write for thirty minutes on these aspects of "my life as a partner." Pay attention to the following questions:

- Which areas of your life surprised you as you wrote about them?
- Which areas of your life are most impacted by your partnership? The least?
- How do you think God feels about your partnership?
- What choices have you made that you would like to discuss/ review with your partner at this time?
- How are you feeling about your role as a partner now?

## Contemplation

The daily intensity of a committed relationship impacts us on many
levels, including the spiritual level. Some long-term relationships that
are smooth-running may seem to fall into patterns of ritual and relating
that are comfortable and require less attention than new relationships.
The challenge then is to choose intimacy and growth. Other relationships are fraught with tension, either overtly or covertly, and take all of
our attention, whether we recognize it or not. The challenge in this case
is to choose authenticity and renewal. Turning our attention to God's
presence within this most intimate and challenging partnership helps
us find ways of infusing, sustaining, healing, and blessing our personal
love with God's love.

- What other resources are available to your partnership? Faith
  community, personal sharing, retreat time together?
- How does your partnership benefit others?
- How do you, or how could you, choose to spend time together
  having fun?
- What aspect of your spiritual journey would you like to share
  with your partner today?

# CHAPTER 31
## Faith Community

Committing to the spiritual path, for some, also means living with and praying with a faith community. While some people choose to walk the path outside of community, having like-minded souls to walk with can offer rich sources of love and compassion and encouragement. Deciding on a community to belong to confronts us with immediate questions: Will we share our spiritual journey with others, and if so, how? Will we accompany others, and allow them to accompany us? Will we do this in the context of a committed, participatory community setting? Or will we choose to forge a more solitary, less structured path? Most religious/faith traditions consider community of one sort or another to be essential, and that will form part of our response to these questions. But considerations will also come into play, such as our need for company, how we feel about ritual and sacramental worship, how comfortable we are with the way we interact with others and they with us, how we feel about the roles and opportunities for participation that are available to us. These are all fruitful questions with no wrong answers—questions that are worth examining as part of our continuing relationship with God.

### Reflection

Think about the faith community in which you are currently a member. If you are not currently a member of any community, reflect on a time when you were. If you have never been a member of a faith tradition or a faith community, is there a faith community image that you hold? Perhaps gleaned from literature or the media, or heard about from friends? Hold this image in your mind. Place yourself in the setting of this faith community, in the midst of a worship service. What does this community setting look like? How is the seating arranged? Who is presiding? Who else is participating? Who is in the congregation? What is the atmosphere like? What kind of lighting is there, what kind of music is played, if any? Where are you standing or sitting? What is your role? How do you feel, physically, mentally, emotionally, spiritually? Be in this place for a few moments, noticing your own sensations. Then extend your noticing out to the rest of the community. Do people seem restless, engaged, or at peace? Notice your response to how the rest of the community is feeling. How does your awareness of others affect your own experience of worship?

- How easily were you able to imagine this setting?
- How did it feel to place yourself within this setting?
- Was there anything you noticed that you don't normally notice?
- What did it feel like to include others in your awareness?
- What aspects of the setting pleased you? What aspects bothered you?

## Pen in Hand

Write about why you have chosen—or would choose—this particular faith community to participate in. Describe how you came to belong and why you stay. Explore your sense of choice. What are the reasons you originally chose this community? If you were to choose again, would you still choose this community? Why? Why not? Include all aspects of these reasons, from the most practical (the church is down the street, the time they offer services suits my schedule) to the most ineffable (something happens when I attend that affects me spiritually). Include your understanding of what your faith tradition has to say about how one chooses a community.

## Noticing

- How important have you found these questions to be in the past?
- How does it feel to reflect on them now?
- What are you learning about your choices as you begin reflecting?
- What made it hard or easy to answer these questions?

## On the Path

Write what it means for you to be in faith community. What are the benefits, and what are the disadvantages? If you are not currently a member

of a faith community or have never been, write about what you imagine
the advantages and disadvantages would be. Spend some time thinking
about and then writing about how you would design your ideal faith
community. What would you change about your current community?
How would you change your own relationship to, or place in, that community? And finally, how does your participation in a faith community
facilitate your relationship with God? Consider these questions:

- Which aspect of faith community do you find the most challenging?
- Are there areas of the community that don't interest you and
  in which you don't participate? What are they? (for instance,
  in service work, in worship attendance, in how much you are
  willing to reveal and share of yourself, in how available you are
  to new members or needy members, etc.)
- What prevents you from fuller participation?
- On what levels are you participating fully?
- Where do you meet God in your faith community?

## Contemplation

The spiritual path is not an isolated one, either from other aspects of
our lives such as career and culture, or from the relationships that we
build and sustain in the everyday world. We learn to love God through
loving others, because the mystery that is God is embodied and expressed through our human affections. We glimpse and experience the
numinous love of God in a more accessible, human form. We grapple
with our own ability to be authentic with God by practicing being ourselves with others; practicing spiritual intimacy on a human scale offers
a model for intimacy with God. We find we grow in faith and spirit
when we commit ourselves to a faith community.

- How are you feeling about your role in your faith community?
- What needs are not being met in your faith community experience?
- What needs are being met?
- How might you bring these feelings and needs to God?

# CHAPTER 32
## Global Community

One day as I sat by the edge of San Francisco Bay, I was momentarily visited by the image of an unknown woman walking toward a well in a desert landscape. I felt connected to this woman, though I knew somehow that she was halfway across the world. This glimpse into the connectedness between the two of us extended, in my heart, to all people walking the earth at that moment, and even to all people who had ever walked the earth. This powerful awareness lasted only a minute or two, but has stayed with me, as a reminder of the global connection of all people, for years.

The spiritual path usually starts with a journey into exploring the self but moves toward communion with all of humanity through the grace of God, as we discover both our uniqueness and our interconnectedness with others. Examining our connection to the global community through the path of social responsibility, a path that invites us into participation with others beyond our immediate circle, enriches our sense of the spirit and strengthens our relationship with God as we learn to care for all of God's people. Moving outward into conscious participation with our brothers and sisters in the human family opens new paths for God's presence and creates new opportunities for transformation, as we step beyond our familiar patterns into the cultural, social, and spiritual vistas that await us in the people we encounter, across the street or around the world. We are all one.

### Reflection

Think about your place on the planet. How do you visualize your own corner of the globe? Begin with the geography: where you live and the conditions you live in. Imagine your home: the room where you spend the most time. See yourself in this room, living your life. Imagine God's presence with you in this room. Move from imagining your home to your neighborhood. Then gradually expand that to an image of your town, your region, your state, your country. How far can you go out into the world in your imagination, stretching the boundaries of your corner of the world, while keeping in mind your own room, your own home? Can you include a country halfway around the world? Can you include a small child in a field in that distant country? Is God still here, in all of these places?

- How far were you able to go in your imagination, while still feeling connected to your own immediate space?
- Which far-off country did you imagine?
- What is your connection with that far-off country?
- How do you feel toward that small child?
- How was it to imagine God in all of these places?

## Pen in Hand

What does your corner of the globe look like? Describe your own setting: your home, neighborhood, town, and region. Stick to the physical details for now. After you have written this brief description, explore connections within your region with other cultures, other faiths, other ways of life that are different from the culture, ethnicity, or faith tradition you operate in. Are there places of worship that are different from yours, that represent other cultures, other parts of the world? Are there communities, stores, or restaurants in your part of the world that represent other regions or nations? What is your relationship to the places and people that represent these other cultures, places, and ways of life?

## Noticing

- What is your level of knowledge about the cultures and faiths that coexist in your own part of the world with you?
- What are your feelings about the amount of diversity within your community, or the lack of it?
- How much have you paid attention to cultures outside your own in the past?
- How do you feel as you reflect on them now?

## On the Path

It is possible to join the spiritual practice and philosophy of social justice with the personal, spiritual path of self-actualization and alignment in God. It depends on our ability to connect with other people, both face-to-face as individuals and in a larger sense as a global, human community. Reflect on how your own faith journey either facilitates or distracts from your ability to connect with and be compassionate with others, both personally and globally. Write about your understanding of what your faith tradition teaches about caring for others, both locally and globally. Then write about how this resonates in your own heart, and how it has played a part in your own experience. Ask yourself:

- How do you feel about what is asked of you by your faith tradition, in terms of recognizing and caring for other people?
- Where do you feel the need to connect with others beyond your immediate family, your immediate community? In what ways might you begin to do that?
- What prevents you from fuller participation in the human family?
- On what levels are you participating fully?
- How might this participation or lack of participation affect your relationship with God?

## Contemplation

So many gifts and adventures await us in the world beyond our own dwellings, our own families, our own communities. If we choose to extend our connections, both externally in terms of social justice work and internally in terms of seeking greater awareness and compassion for all people, we are granted the opportunity to love and to learn from the wisdom, creativity, and courage of others. We make room for the spirit by opening our hearts and our minds to others. In doing so we extend God's reach and reach toward God ourselves.

- How are you feeling about your place in the world?
- What needs could you help meet in your community?
- Where do you feel drawn to seek greater connection and to offer service?
- What do you feel God is inviting you to do?

# Section 6
# *Mapping the World of Work*

*We are the agents of the Creative Spirit in this world. Real advance in the spiritual life, then, means accepting this vocation with all it involves. Not merely turning over the pages of an engineering magazine and enjoying the pictures, but putting on overalls and getting on with the job.*
—Evelyn Underhill, *The Spiritual Life*

Is your work something you escape from, eager to get on with the real business of living? Or is work something you escape to, seeking the solace and challenges offered by your workplace and your professional role? Perhaps work is an integral part of your whole life journey, an expression of who you are and what you value: neither an escape from or to anything, but a mindful choice based on deep spiritual fulfillment. Regardless, most adults are engaged in work of one kind or another for most of their adult lives. Examining how and why we work offers a way to more clearly know ourselves and to understand how the spirit permeates our working lives. Do you work to pay the bills, to exercise your talents and gifts, or to be of service? Fortunately, work can be an opportunity to combine all three aspects of responsible and enjoyable adulthood: financial sustainability, creativity, and giving to others. In this section we will explore many aspects of our place in the world of work, vocation, and creativity, including: why and how we do the work we have chosen, what other possibilities might exist for us in our working lives, and how God plays a part in our working identity.

# CHAPTER 33
## My Current Work

Work is a necessary feature of adult life, unless we are financially independent; even then many people still choose to engage in work of some kind. Whether work is undertaken by choice or an unavoidable necessity, it occupies much of our precious time and mental, physical, and emotional energy. How is your spirit engaged in these tasks? It seems, at times, that God is absent from the workday, but God meets us in every aspect of life, not just in sacred settings. How do we find God's presence in this vital aspect of our adult selves?

### Reflection

Think about your current work situation, whether that be a job or lack of one. If you are retired, think about the last job you held, or any volunteer work you are currently doing. If you have never worked but would like to or are thinking about entering the workforce, then use this time to envision work as you would like it to be.

Let yourself be in "work mode" in your imagination. Visualize your place of work. What does it look like? Do you have a space of your own at work? How is your own space set up? Is there a view? What is the lighting like, and the sound level? How do you feel in this space? Are you working with others or alone? As you imagine yourself working in your usual setting, what is the general atmosphere? What is your usual mental and emotional state at work? How do you feel physically? Notice all you can about who you are and how you feel at work.

- What is it like to visit your workplace in your imagination?
- How do you feel about the physical environment?
- How do you feel about the people or lack of people?
- Which aspects of your workplace please you?
- Which aspects of your workplace bother you?

## Pen in Hand

Reflect on yourself within the work environment. How would you describe yourself in terms not just of job effectiveness or performance, but in terms of who you are as a person? What qualities do you bring to your work? Does your work engage all of your gifts? Are there gifts you can't use at work? Write for fifteen minutes on your work identity, describing both the positive and the negative aspects of how you present yourself and how you immerse yourself in your work. As you write, think about and include how these qualities pertain to your spiritual identity. How does your work identity express or fulfill who you are spiritually? How does it impede or disrupt who you are spiritually? Try to avoid making judgments about how spiritual you are at work. Just name how your work identity either facilitates or impedes your relationship with God. Understanding how we present ourselves and who we are at work can help us move closer to a more authentic expression of ourselves in the workplace.

## Noticing

- In which situations or settings were you able to identify your spiritual self?
- What is it like to think about God in the context of your work?
- What surprises you about what you wrote?
- What feelings does this exercise bring up?

## On the Path

Write a narrative to God, focusing on who you are in relation to your work. Include the joys and rewards, as well as the tensions inherent in your current work situation. Stay with present reality, as opposed to writing about the work you would rather have or hope to have in the future. (We will focus on future work aspirations in the next chapter.) Write about positive and negative things that are tangible, such as "I get to be creative, I don't like the way I act around my coworkers, I like being able to support myself, I am so tired at the end of the day." What are the challenges? When are you bored? When are you stimulated and enthused? How would you describe your connections with others? How does work challenge you? In what way does work draw you closer to or further away from God? Ask yourself and write about:

- What is your current level of work satisfaction?
- What spiritual gifts are you receiving right now, in the midst of your current work situation? What gifts are you giving?
- Where is God in your work?
- How might you invite God to help you resolve and transform any boredom, anger, tension, or anxiety related to your work?
- Where do you see opportunities for "work as a spiritual practice"?
- How does it feel to think about including God in the thoughts, feelings, and experiences you have about your work?

## Contemplation

Circumstances beyond our control often impact many aspects of our work, from who we work with to the kinds of tasks we accomplish. What we can always choose, however, is how we will be with God in the midst of our work. We can practice the awareness of our relationship with God in the midst of work, in the center of our work identity, and as we walk our career or vocational paths. Writing to God about how we feel and who we are as working adults helps us stay awake to what we most want and how we most want to be in alignment with God.

- How are you feeling about your work identity?
- What about your workplace brings you the most joy? How might you convey that to God and to others?
- What about your work or workplace would you most like to change? How might God be a part of that process?

# CHAPTER 34
## Seeking My Calling

What does the idea of "a calling" mean to you? Does it mean being drawn to a role in ministry, or a helping profession, or perhaps even to a creative life as an artist or writer? These may all be "callings," or they may not: the concept of call is more about the process of finding and fulfilling our heart's desire and living an authentic life than the type of work we do. Someone may be called to be a harbormaster; someone else may be called to be a nurse, or run a clothing store. Seeking our calling means locating the place where our gifts and talents match a need in the world, and by fulfilling that need, we are in alignment with ourselves and with God. Manifesting our calling means we enter the world, seeking honorable work.

Jobs, tasks, forms of ministry, interactions aimed at solving problems, caretaking, and projects of every kind are all containers that constitute what we mean by "work." Our work is the outward manifestation of our energies, creativity, desires, and personal needs. For many of us, our current work fulfills important aspects of our creative and spiritual selves as well as sustaining us financially, and we are filled with gratitude for the blessings our work brings us. We feel called to be exactly where we are. For others of us, we may find that after reflecting on and examining our current work situation, we feel called to something more than we are able to realize or to accomplish in our current circumstances. This chapter addresses those seeking their calling, while the next chapter addresses those people who are seeking to deepen and expand their calling.

If you are still seeking your calling, then you want and need work that asks more of you and allows you fuller expression of your creativity, your gifts, and your values than your current situation offers. How do we get from our current situation to this new reality? We can start with imagining what this new kind of work and this new workplace would look like if we could create it ourselves. We start by cocreating with God a vision that we then move toward, through practical application and through prayer.

## Reflection

Is there a kind of work that you have always hungered after? Something that you have dreamed about but set aside or chose not to pursue for various reasons? What kind of work that others engage in inspires envy? Envy provides a clue about what you long for, though sometimes the clue is disguised. For instance, we may envy someone famous, when what we long for is not fame but to be heard. We may envy someone in a position of authority, when what we long for is not the position itself but the ability to effect meaningful change. What do you long for? Do you seek more autonomy, or a congenial community? Do you wish to use your intellect, engage your body, assume leadership, play with children, or reason with colleagues? Think about the qualities of the work you would choose if you had complete freedom to make the choice and why these qualities attract you.

- What new aspects of your longing have you noticed?
- What feelings are stirred in you by thinking about what you long for in terms of work?
- Are there any connections with your current work and work that you desire?
- Can you imagine any path that would lead you toward this new work?
- How might it be to bring your longing for new work to God?

**Pen in Hand**

Write out every aspect of the kind of work that you would most like to have. That list can include qualities or features of your current work if you find it satisfying. Include not only the kind of work you would like, but the setting, the hours, the people you'd like to work with or for, and the pay or other compensation. Design your ideal work and your ideal workplace without worrying about whether such a position is possible.

**Noticing**

- How long have you thought about the work and the workplace you described? Is this an ongoing desire or a relatively new one?
- What feelings arose as you thought about this ideal work?
- How does it feel to imagine yourself doing this work, in this setting?
- What is your level of knowledge about the kind of work you are describing?

**On the Path**

The work we most desire may or may not be available to us; a variety of circumstances can block the way forward. Training, skill levels, family or financial considerations, and even our own sense of self-worth can get in the way—permanently or temporarily—of seeking out the perfect work. These roadblocks can cause despair, frustration, and may result in denial about how important these longings are for our creative, emotional, physical, and spiritual well-being. When all practical solutions have been explored and failed, we can offer our longings and hopes about meaningful work to God. Spend some time centering on how you feel about the work you have envisioned for yourself. Allow yourself to fully experience the desire you have for this work. Then imagine yourself bringing this desire to God. Spend as much time as you need, writing to God about your desire, your fears, your frustrations, and your hopes. You might want to also address:

- Do you feel you need to justify this desire? Why? What about this desire feels like it requires justification in God's eyes?
- How would this new work affect your sense of self?
- How would this new work help you to feel closer to God?
- What gifts would you be able to express in this new work?
- What other spiritual values might be expressed?

## Contemplation

Because work plays such a major role in the lives of most of us every day (though its importance is not necessarily based on how much time we actually spend on it), we may forget that it is not all "up to us" to figure out how to bring our longings for meaning, effectiveness, creativity, and commitment into alignment with the work we have been given or the work we long to do. Inviting God into the process is not like consulting with a career counselor, but is more like making the connection between our desire and God's desire. In the process, we may be led to a new way of being in the world of work that we could not have imagined or invented on our own.

- How are you feeling about the work you have imagined for yourself?
- Along with prayer, what practical steps might you begin to take to realize your vision, no matter how small?
- Who might you share these dreams with, who will listen and not judge?
- What do you feel God is inviting you to do?

# CHAPTER 35
## Manifesting My Calling in New Ways

Finding a place in the world of work, like finding a mate or a place to live, would seem to be the culmination of a sustained and important journey. And, indeed, it is; but just as the journey ends in a sense of coming home to where we belong, new paths begin to open up. Questions arise: How can I expand this call into other aspects of my life? What do I need to nourish my spirit and renew my energy? What new ways of manifesting my call are still unexplored? While committing to the identity and purpose that answering the call entails, we still seek more.

### Reflection

A friend of mine answered the call to become a writer many years ago. She has written several books since then, published several articles. Yet she still grapples with her calling. Not the basic question of "should I be a writer" but more subtle, nuanced questions that nevertheless hold her attention: How is my writing serving others? What direction will I go in next with my writing? What topics might I be avoiding? How might I grow as a writer? These questions can be translated to fit the journey for all who are called, not just writers. Ask yourself:

- How is my calling serving others, and why is that important to me?
- What new direction might I go in next within my calling? What attracts me?

- What might I be avoiding in my work? What might be holding me back from evolving?
- What new talents or skills might enhance my ability to fulfill my calling?
- How might God be inviting me to fulfill my calling in new ways?

## Pen in Hand

Write about a challenge that was presented to you recently or is currently before you in your work. Something that asks you to move beyond your current arena, your current comfort level. This may be a new assignment, or a new way to relate to someone you work with, or a new way of defining your calling. What is it about this challenge that appeals to you? What is it about this challenge that troubles you or makes you hesitate?

## Noticing

- How long have you been pondering this challenge?
- What appeals to you about this new possibility?
- What feelings arise when you think about responding to this new challenge?
- How do you feel about being challenged, about being presented with new opportunities in your calling?

## On the Path

People who have found a way to fulfill their sense of call bring many gifts to the world. They offer hope for those still seeking. Their enthusiasm for their work enlivens every interaction and shines through in their work. And as this enthusiasm and hope shines forth, it both enlightens others and brings blessings in return, as this same enthusiasm and hope springs forth in others and spreads abundance. How might you, as someone who feels like they are in the right place doing the right work, offer your experience, strength, and hope for others who are still finding their way? How might you give back to the world that has provided you with a way to fulfill your call and manifest your gifts?

Write about how you can share your blessings with others. In what form, with what means, might you extend a helping hand to those who still seek? Write about:

- What can you directly do to share your blessings?
- How would sharing your blessings affect your own calling?
- How would sharing your gifts and your wisdom impact your relationship with God?
- What holds you back from extending yourself to others?
- What kinds of support most helped you in your own search for fulfillment?

## Contemplation

Giving back what we have received creates a perpetual cycle of giving and receiving, growth and renewal. Sometimes we can get stuck in our calling; because we don't have to spend energy seeking, because we have settled in, we forget that seeking also brings the reward of new vision, new experience, and new energy. Helping others to seek and to find rekindles the fires of exploration and new adventure. We reconnect with what it felt like to begin the journey with enthusiasm and hope.

- What new challenges might arise if you were to help others find their way?
- Along with prayer, what practical steps might you begin to take to renew your own sense of call?
- Who might you invite to share this work of helping others?
- How might God want you to proceed?

# CHAPTER 36
## Spirituality and Creativity

Creativity, like spirituality, infuses every aspect of our being, though it may appear in different guises and be expressed in various ways, from the esoteric to the everyday. Creativity exists in all we do, at work, in relationships, at home, or in our general attitude toward life. It doesn't exist only in those considered to be "artists." Noticing it and embracing it helps us remain open, flexible, and inventive in the midst of life's challenges and opportunities.

### Reflection

If someone were to say to you, "oh, you are so creative!" what might they be referring to? Hold that thought in your mind and enjoy it. If the only thought that comes to mind is "I'm not creative at all" then try to expand your sense of creativity. Think beyond the world of the arts and crafts. Cooking, gardening, fixing things, solving problems, or even serving on committees that need ideas and input are all creative ventures. How about the ways you have devised to cope with your life, to handle crises, to make major decisions? These all require an element of creativity. Imagine a time when you used creative energy to transform something, whether it be words, objects, a situation, or yourself, into something new. How did that feel? How often have you been able to call on this creative spirit in your life? Are there any areas of life where this creative energy has been particularly fruitful or helpful? What was that like, and how do you feel about that experience now?

- How would you define your creative self?
- Did you think of areas of creativity that surprised you?
- How do you feel about your creativity?
- How important is creativity to you?
- What do you believe God's role is in creativity?

## Pen in Hand

If you could express your creativity in any way, what would it be? How would you ground your creative energy in a concrete form, something that you could engage in with your mind, body, and spirit? Don't hamper your thoughts with practical concerns like money, time, or talent. Write about this creative outlet, describing the materials, the setting, the projects, every aspect of this creative work that appeals to you. Would you like to design a worship service? Change your personal style? Take pictures? Decorate your home? Create sacred spaces? Have you harbored dreams of building your own boat, designing a website, or making quilts? This dream doesn't need to be practical or even meaningful: it may seem frivolous or ludicrous. Write about it anyway.

## Noticing

- How did it feel to write about this creative outlet?
- What did you discover as you wrote?
- How private has this creative dream been?
- What would it be like to share this creative dream with God?

## On the Path

Now that you have written about a creative outlet you have long wanted to pursue, write about what prevents you from embarking on the creative journey. You may have practical concerns like needing money for the materials or not enough time available. Issues such as self-worth, or lack of ability or talent are important to list here. As you write, offer these feelings and these concerns to God. Keep your heart open to possibility. Seemingly immovable barriers or unanswerable concerns are sometimes transformed when explored in God's presence. The very act of prayerful writing means that you are describing something that may find new hope, new ways of seeing and acting, in God. You are creatively approaching God though your writing, and in so doing you open the door for God to create in you anew. If a new way of seeing or feeling about creativity comes to mind, write that down as well. Offer to God, in your writing:

- The feeling at the heart of your desire to create
- Your hope for a creative life
- Your desire to move beyond any negative messages, or to create in spite of them
- Your willingness to explore new ways of being creative

## Contemplation

Choosing to create is choosing to matter, to care, to invest ourselves, to commit, to enter into a partnership with the Holy, creative spirit. In so doing we make ourselves vulnerable on many levels. Asking God to witness and cocreate with us in this adventure helps us to keep our hearts open to creative possibility, and gives us the courage and endurance needed for the creative journey.

- How are you feeling about your desire to create?
- What resources might you draw on as you explore this new territory?
- How might you bring this desire to God, to a friend, or your community?

## PART III

# For Further Exploration

*In this next part I have included information on writing for others and finding and forming a creative community. As the novelist Colette once said, "Writing only leads to more writing," which to me sounds like a celebration of the reality that once we begin this transformative practice, we find ourselves drawn to continue.*

# If You Want to Write about
# Spirituality for Others

*After exploring the chapters in this book, you may find yourself wanting to keep writing, and to eventually move your writing practice out into the world to share with others. There are many good resources for learning how to write for others, and you will find some listed in the appendix. You may wish to begin by reading this brief reflection on spiritual writing and doing the writing exercises.*

Writers of spirituality explore how, or why, or for whom spiritual experience happens, sometimes in esoteric circumstances, and more often, in daily life. They are concerned with awareness, which includes being aware of their own self, the world around them and beyond, and their relationship to the Sacred, by whatever name they call it. Take time to consider who you are as a spiritual person, because it will be reflected (hopefully!) in your writing. More than any other writing genre, spiritual writing reveals the writer to the reader, offering a meaningful connection that both the writer and the reader hope and long for. Knowing something about your spiritual identity becomes a necessary factor in conveying your experience, because the way you choose to tell your story will be more effective if you are being true to who you are and what you believe. This knowledge of your spiritual identity includes any beliefs or even biases you hold about your religious tradition or other religious traditions, because although you may choose to write about spirituality as separate from religion, these two arenas of experience often overlap and interconnect.

For instance, if you want to present yourself as a writer operating from a particular faith tradition, you will most likely draw on the images, language, literary, and cultural references of your tradition, and your orientation will be clear to everyone. Or, you may be a writer who wishes to operate outside of the confines of a particular tradition. Or perhaps you wish to write from a specific religious perspective, but you want to open the doors of that tradition wide enough to allow others to experience what it has to offer. In all cases, you will still need to pay attention to how your spiritual identity has been shaped and formed, for it will show through in your writing, from the metaphors you choose to the conclusions you draw, whether you consciously choose to write about your religious background and identity, or not. Spiritual writing should (hopefully) move beyond an attitude of "preaching to the choir" (notice my use of a religious cliché here!) with the goal of conveying an experience of the spirit to as many receptive readers as possible. A couple of suggestions follow for freeing your writing from hidden obstacles to understanding.

## Avoid Religious Jargon

Every tradition has words that are known only or mostly to its members. While jargon can be a helpful shortcut in conveying information to those who are "in the know," it tends to push readers away because they either have an automatic reaction to these words, or they miss much of your meaning. Unfamiliar words or phrases that pertain to the worship service, certain types of esoteric knowledge, or more obscure historical references should be explained. For instance, would non-Catholics (or many Catholics, for that matter) know what an "ambo" is? If you want to write for a larger audience, then check your writing for these references or better yet, have someone read your work who is not familiar with your tradition. Do they still "get it?"

## Avoid Lecturing

People are more easily attracted by stories than by lectures, and by openness than by rigidity. Think of your own experiences in school. Which teachers held your attention, those who stood at the front of the class and recited or harangued, or those who engaged you in story and conversation, respecting your own perceptions and insights? If you want to convey an insight or an experience that feels so important and true that you are compelled to try and express yourself in writing, then let that passion show, but don't tell people that they must respond the same way, or chances are, they will draw back. The same basic rule for fiction, "show, don't tell," holds true in spiritual writing. Show people what you feel and/or believe, don't lecture them on what they should feel or believe. Lecturing or "preaching" in your writing will narrow your audience considerably.

## Naming Your Experience

Even the writers who work firmly within their traditions, who leave no doubt as to their religious orientation, are most successful at expressing the spiritual when they use images and language that venture beyond the familiar, into images and words that open up new ways of thinking about and imagining the spirit. God invites us, through the gift of creativity, to venture into uncharted waters in our imaginations as we seek new ways to describe the ineffable. We may not be able to name or describe God once and for all, but the process of trying is just as, if not more, important; because trying to describe God means we are engaged in trying to get closer to God. We are at play in the fields of the heart, in the presence of the spirit. Try this exercise as a way to begin playing at naming God. Let your creative spirit go free.

### Exercise 1: Naming Your Experience

Make a list of twenty words for God. Stretch yourself: try for images you have not used, read, or written before. Use your imagination, your experience, and your creative gifts. When you have made this list (don't stop before twenty words—when you push beyond your limits you may surprise yourself), take the one word or phrase that resonates the most for you, and write a paragraph or two that more fully explores this image. Then write about what you learned about yourself and how you imagine God.

## Who Is Your Audience?

Let's say you have been asked to read some of your spiritual writing to a roomful of interested listeners. Who is sitting in the chairs in the room? What faith tradition are they from? What is their general attitude, what other kinds of books do they read? And more importantly, are these the people you most want to reach, that you most want to connect with? These are the people that you will have in mind as you write, even though they may not consciously appear in your mind's eye at the time. When we write, we have something to say, but we also have someone we want to say it to. This may be as narrow a group as a parent or spouse, or as large as the whole world. Who are you writing for, and why?

*Exercise 2: Who Is Your Audience?*

Write a brief portrait of your ideal reader. What do you like about them? Why do you need to reach them? How can you reach those readers? Then describe readers who won't share your perspective. Do you still want to reach this person or this group? How might you do that?

## How Will You Reach Your Audience?

While the exercises in this book have focused on writing for yourself as you also write to God, choosing to write for others means making a practical assessment of the markets available to you for your work. Investigating the publishing marketplace is a realistic, unavoidable aspect of having your work read, unless you only wish to write for friends and family. The Internet is a rich source of information, not only for finding out about print publications and publishers, but for finding online markets as well. Because there are so many venues available, you will need to spend some time figuring out which markets you wish to try and write for. Use as a starting point those publications and websites that most attract you, that are most in alignment with your own spiritual identity. Find the markets that match your spirit, your talent, and your writing style, rather than trying to make your spiritual identity and your writing fit the market.

*Exercise 3: How Will You Reach Your Audience?*

Think about the spiritual publications that attract you and answer the following questions for yourself.

- What is it about these publications that makes you want to write for them?
- How much will you have to tailor what you believe or the way you write to fit their style?
- What is your overall goal, both spiritually and in your career, in writing for these markets?

By choosing to enter the world of publishing as a writer of spirituality, you are opening up your spiritual process to the world. Seek out other writers who can support and encourage you toward your goal of writing for others. They can be a buffer against the harsher realities of the literary marketplace, so that you may be free to stay open to the spirit as you write. Know that being called to write is not the same as being published: one is a movement of the heart, and the other is a combination of a set of circumstances, timing, and practical realities. These two aspects of being published, the mystical and the practical, do not always coincide. Regardless, the process of writing about your spiritual journey will lead you closer to God: the ultimate listener, the most receptive audience of all.

# Finding and/or Forming
## a Creative Community

Communities formed with the intention of supporting members on their creative path are thriving these days, both in physical settings such as retreat centers and on the Internet. Writers, healers, artists, and spiritual directors, although supported by God's presence, mostly work in a solitary relationship with either their client or their art. Intentional community, or community formed in a spirit of *intention* rather than of bare necessity or imposed requirements, helps ease the isolation and recharge the spirit.

Forming a community where it is safe to talk about the process of doing one's work can provide invaluable support, group energy, and wisdom. Many writing groups band together in order to share their actual work, in addition to talking about the creative process. They critique, offer marketing suggestions, and share tips on everything from the craft of fiction to writing a successful cover letter. Other groups focus on sharing the experience of doing their work, whether they write, sculpt, paint, direct, or counsel. These are all creative acts, requiring our best selves and our core energy. A group that joins together to support each other and share in the mystery that is creativity can go beyond discussing the practicalities of producing work or producing results, and move into recognizing and celebrating the life experience of each participant as a creative mystery, continually unfolding.

Groups can be formed online or in person. Online groups usually set up as e-mail discussion groups. Online communities allow members to reach across boundaries of time and space: one of my own groups has members from Chicago to New Zealand. Seek out members by using trusted sources of referral: often recommendations by friends or co-creatives are the best. Start thinking about who you might like to get to know on a deeper level. Look for the qualities that you admire and use your intuition to guide you.

Set guidelines from the start which address the goal and vision of the group. Will you have a closed membership? If you invite others to join, how will you as a group decide on who you want to ask to join? Are there any creative criteria for joining, such as how serious you are about your craft? A group that consists of artists in different genres can be a great way to get fresh perspective on the creative process, so don't feel you must limit your group to writers, or writers of one genre. Usually groups of between five and eight members work best: more than two or three allows for variety and more than eight risks becoming too impersonal. Remember, these kinds of groups are based on the creative process itself, not on what you produce. Proceed by consensus, and if the atmosphere gets at all toxic, address it immediately. Topics such as creative rhythms, creativity and the spirit, incorporating your creativity into your daily life, feeling blocked or restless or frustrated are all good topics for group conversation, because we all know what it's like and can offer sympathy, insights, and support. The group doesn't need to be about problem solving; it can be based on a common sense of "We are all in this together." That shared feeling goes a long way toward dispelling isolation and despair. It can also be a place to celebrate the victories that others might not appreciate, such as the day you resisted cleaning out the fridge and wrote instead; how you stayed centered in a chaotic situation; or how you have come to believe that you are a "real" artist, no matter what anyone says.

A shared set of values among group members is more important than the kinds or amounts of work produced by its members. Do you want a group based on a shared creative philosophy that addresses issues of integrity, ethics, and meaning as they apply to the creative life? Or are you more interested in letting some controversy stir the collective pot? Above all, remember that you are giving yourself the gift of taking your creative life seriously when you meet with others to focus on what it is that moves us to walk the creative path.

## Questions to Consider and Write About

- Describe your own ideal creative community.
- What are three steps you could take toward making that community a reality?
- What are your goals as a member of such a community?
- What goals do you envision for the community as a whole?

# For Further Reading: Suggested Resources on Writing and Spirituality

## Autobiography and Memoir

Phifer, Nan. *Memoirs of the Soul: Writing Your Spiritual Autobiography.* Cincinnati, OH: Walking Stick Press, 2002.
Wakefield, Dan. *The Story of Your Life: Writing a Spiritual Autobiography.* Boston: Beacon Press, 1990.

## Creative Writing Books that Include a Spiritual Perspective

Aronie, Nancy Slonin. *Writing from the Heart: Tapping the Power of Your Inner Voice.* New York: Hyperion Books, 1998.
Goldberg, Natalie. *Writing Down the Bones.* Boston: Shambhala, 1986.
Lamott, Anne. *Bird By Bird.* New York: Random House/Anchor Books Division, 1994.

## Creative Writing Books from a Christian Perspective

L'Engle, Madeleine. *Walking on Water: Reflections on Faith and Art.* New York: North Point Press, 1995.
Sayers, Dorothy. *The Mind of the Maker.* San Francisco: HarperSanFrancisco, 1941; reprint, 1987.